Depression and Intense Anxieties Your Quickest Way Out

A Survivor's True Account

Rose C. Manalo

Depression and Intense Anxieties:
Your Quickest Way Out
A Survivor's True Account
By Rose Manalo
Published by Neverbound Publishing House
74 Bel Air Drive, Cor. Fremont St., Laguna Bel Air 1, Don Jose,
Sta. Rosa City, Laguna, Region 4-A, Philippines
Twitter @rosecmanalo1
Instagram @rosecmanalo1
Facebook www.facebook.com/rosecmanalo1
Email rosalinamanalo1970@yahoo.com

Book cover image and design:
by Rose C. Manalo

Scriptures marked AMP are taken from the AMPLIFIED BIBLE (AMP):
Scripture taken from the AMPLIFIED® BIBLE, Copyright © 1954, 1958, 1962,
1964, 1965, 1987 by the Lockman Foundation Used by Permission.
(www.Lockman.org)

Scriptures marked TLB are taken from the THE LIVING BIBLE (TLB):
Scripture taken from THE LIVING BIBLE copyright© 1971. Used by
permission of Tyndale House Publishers, Inc., Carol Stream, Illinois 60188.
All rights reserved

Medical Disclaimer:
All information, content, and material in this book is for informational purposes
only and are not intended to serve as a substitute for the consultation, diagnosis,
and/or medical treatment of a qualified physician or healthcare provider.

ISBN
Softbound/Paperback: 978-621-8153-01-1

"Illnesses do not come upon us out of the blue. They are developed from small daily sins against Nature. When enough sins have accumulated, illnesses will suddenly appear."
Hippocrates (Father of Modern Medicine)

3 John 2 Amplified Bible (AMP)
Beloved, I pray that in every way you may succeed and prosper and be in good health [physically], just as [I know] your soul prospers [spiritually].

For my Mama
Sianing Canlas
and my mother-in-law
Menchie Hawkings

ACKNOWLEDGMENTS

Yes, it's true that the years 2008-2010 were the most horrible years of my life. I am most thankful to God for letting me have those years. It's easy to consider the many other diseases I could have suffered from had I not first suffered from depression. I now look at my experience with depression as an efficient braking mechanism. It was the perfect "pit stop" - meant to show me the damages my own actions have done. It gave me a chance to apply the necessary repairs: physically, emotionally, mentally and spiritually.

The knowledge I gained about depression helped the rest of my family. Next to me, it helped our son Jetross, dodge depression and lose 55 pounds in less than a year. It also helped so many of my friends and relatives connect their ill-health - mental and physical - to the poor quality of nutrients they've relied on for decades.

And now it is helping you. Please help others by spreading the word.

I am eternally grateful to my mother; whose creativity I've seen unmatched by anyone I know. Thank you, Mama, for showing me by example how to create something out of seemingly hopeless pieces. You have done so without complaining but with plain stubborn focus until the job was done. Alzheimer's had clouded this wonderful version of you, but it will always remain in my heart and mind.

A very special thanks to my very good friend Jennifer Ilano, for accepting my request to copy-edit this book. Reading the refined chapters encouraged me to express my thoughts freely knowing that Jen was there to re-arrange my jumbled sentences and chop off what's unnecessary and redundant (see what happens without Jen's editing?). Whatever redundancies remained are completely my fault.

I would like to thank my family for their patience, love and loads of understanding during the 18 months I needed to write the book. My thanks to my sons Jetcarl and Jetross for being my soundboards when I needed some ruthless opinions and for cheering me on whenever I needed a boost. Your kisses and embraces and "I love you's" truly kept me going. I love you JETS so much.

Lastly... as I write these words, I can smell bacon, eggs and ham being prepared by my husband for my brunch. For today's brunch and the many other meals you've prepared for me, for your quiet patience as well as when you couldn't be, for taking on my role as mother to two demanding sons, and for overcoming something seemingly insurmountable, I thank my dear husband Jet. I love you SHLD.

✳ ✳ ✳

WHO SHOULD READ THIS BOOK?

This book is for the person:

1. who is so sure that tomorrow can only be worse than today
2. who can laugh a lot (or a little) but cannot wait to be alone
3. who thinks her life's purpose is purposeless
4. who feels he is drowning in his own mistakes
5. who thinks there's no safer place than her bedroom
6. who thinks she's incapable of doing anything right
7. who wants to forgive but can't see the point
8. who thinks he's incapable of giving genuine love
9. who finds it hard to trust anyone
10. who dreads meeting new people
11. who feels always fatigued; has weak or numb arms and legs; hears his heart's pounding 24/7; has perpetual upset stomach: constantly takes deep breaths
12. who often feels something bad is about to happen
13. who is always ahead or behind - never here and now
14. who is surrounded by clutter and dust
15. who doesn't appreciate having visitors
16. who is uncomfortable with small talk
17. who has constant mental replays of the "worst" parts
18. who has plenty but feels empty

Depression is not a respecter of fame, security, civil or social status, race, age, gender or even wealth and success. Recent news of suicide by significant personalities give credence to this statement.

How about faith?

I am personally aware that even some people of strong faith have suffered from depression. My own faith in God, despite my severe depression and its harrowing manifestations, was never shaken at any time throughout those three debilitating years.

To some, that statement may sound incongruous, or plain ironic. It "felt" ironic to me to be constantly weak, exhausted, and in dreadful panic, but at the same time, I know with certainty that my eternal salvation was secured no matter what I was going through in this temporal life. That knowledge - that assurance about my personal standing with God - was as real to me as the horrific characteristics of depression: constant forebodings, 24/7 palpitations, insomnia, extreme pessimism, general body weakness, sudden inability to feel happiness, and that perpetual physical "knife" pain in my chest.

However, it was that faith which assured me, that if the Lord wills it, He could heal me instantly through a miracle. But when it became apparent that He had in mind another way of healing for me, it was my faith in God that kept me anchored and daily whispered to me to "wait it out".

So, then what is this common denominator among depression sufferers? What is it that depression sufferers all have? What "qualified" us to be depressed?

This underlying qualifier is our "Heel of Achilles". It is our common vulnerability. It is **the key** to defeating this mental plague. And its elusive face is revealed in this book.

If you have ticked off even just 2 out of the 18 symptoms I listed above, then you most likely have this Heel of Achilles - this particular weakness - as well.

This   book   is   then   for   you.

CONTENTS

CHAPTER 1:
INTRODUCTION

HOW IT ALL FELT LIKE

The years 2008 to 2010 were the most horrible years of my life.

For most of that period, I couldn't feel joy or happiness. I couldn't understand what made people laugh or smile. I was constantly nervous. My chest felt like it had a knife perpetually stuck in my heart. My knees felt like jelly and I walked close to the walls, grabbing furniture to keep myself from collapsing onto the floor.

Every day at 2am, I was jolted awake from sleep. It didn't matter how late I slept; I was awake at 2am and couldn't go back to sleep anymore. For me, those morning hours were the most difficult part of the day. I was the only one up; I couldn't talk to anyone. That early unbroken silence made everything seem darker.

As my depression progressed, I became highly reactive, in an increasingly paralyzing way. I felt dread whenever there were sudden sounds like the ringing of my cellphone, objects falling, cats fighting, or just when someone called out my name.

I didn't like having visitors no matter how well-meaning they were. I did my best to be gracious when we had guests, but my heart palpitated so much more during those times and my fingers and feet felt weaker.

I especially didn't like it when I had to retell the events leading to my depression. A fresh, exposed wound being sliced and re-sliced is how I felt every time I had to discuss our story.

HOW I GOT INTO THE DEPRESSION PIT

By 2007 my husband had been an overseas worker for 7 years. In September of that year, we bought a bakery franchise and put up our bakery. We used up all our savings and even borrowed for more capital.

We were very hopeful and had no reason to doubt that our biggest venture would be a success. However, being a franchise bakery, we were bound to use the premixes sold by our franchisor. After just one month of operation, the premixes resulted in very poor breads and this had gone on for weeks and brought down our sales. After only 3 months in business, we fell heavily in debt and unable to pay our staff, our rent and utilities.

To stop the financial bleeding, I closed the bakery and transferred the equipment from the bakery site to our rented house.

In just a few months we went from being optimistic of the future by having a business of our own, to having nothing in our bank account, and neck-deep in financial debt. We were totally in the red!

One night in January of 2008, after dismissing the last of our bakery staff, and padlocked the bakery, driving home, I could feel the sound of my heart pounding in my chest. My breathing was heavy and frequent, and I couldn't seem to have enough air. Then my hands started to shake while I gripped the stirring wheel. My knees lost their strength and felt like jelly. By God's grace alone, I made it home safely. But that night was the start of my 3-year journey through hell on earth.

Two years into my depression, I was approached by a friend. She was struggling with depression for more than 5 years. She encouraged me to set an appointment with her psychiatrist. She also insisted that I start taking anti-depressants. For both of her suggestions I gave a very tight NO. I told her we couldn't afford it. We didn't have money to spare for therapy nor for any expensive anti-depressant medications.

A year after her visit, I was healed from depression. A year after my healing, my friend committed suicide. I was not able to relay to her the tools I used to free myself from depression.

Those tools are in this book, for you or anyone you know who is suffering from depression.

TOOLS THAT WORK

There are three reasons that we have been repeatedly given as the top "causes" of depression: genes, too much stress and chemical imbalance. Expensive interventions were formulated based on these assumptions. If these treatments were truly founded on sound science, how is it that we now see the steepest ever rise in suicide? And the same fast increase in various forms of incapacity due to depression. This so-called "mental" plague has reached such proportions at a period when anti-depressants are now among the best-selling drugs of all time.

To try to heal depression by using an ineffective tool is not much different from when I tried to deal with my asthma. I took asthma drugs and inhalers; nothing worked because I kept eating foods with very strong allergens such as yellow food coloring. This food dye called "tartrazine" is a very potent asthma allergen that causes inflammation in the gut's lining. My asthma attacks stopped after I avoided consuming foods with tartrazine. **I dealt with the root of the problem: the inflammation in my gut**. But it all started when I came across that piece of information which I used as an effective tool for me to heal from asthma.

In the same way, I am certain that the tools I laid out in this book can help anyone with depression, because they deal with the ROOT of it all: the health of this "shell" we call body. And it starts **with the health of our gut.**

Depression is the "megaphone" the body uses to send you an urgent message. It is its desperate "call to action". It is trying to make you turn and look at its "bill of materials". When we give the body all the right raw materials it needs, it knows what to do with them and how to heal itself.

When the gut starts to heal, the very first changes you will feel is the lifting up and then disappearance of those terrifying sensations of foreboding that have hounded you. **You will immediately notice the difference**. And that is only the beginning. Soon you will be reacquainted with the familiar feelings of hopefulness, contentedness, happiness, enjoyment and even glee. But nothing that we have temporarily lost is desired more than peace, and that too will rekindle in you.

You don't have to wait to be cancer-free, or diabetes-free, arthritis-free, or generally problem-free, before you can be free from depression. You just have to start with one thing and somewhere. Let the next chapter lead you.

Allow this book to shatter the stubborn dogma that you have perceived for decades regarding mental health. When you do, you will find that the process of healing from depression is easy, inexpensive, very practical, satisfying, liberating and most of all, delicious.

CHAPTER 2: MIND YOUR GUT

When I slid down the pit of depression, I had not the slightest idea that our digestive health, particularly our "gut" (large intestines), can directly influence our mental and emotional condition. I had thought that whatever food I ate and digested was eventually excreted, leaving behind the extracted nutrients for the benefit of my "physical" body alone.

How wrong I was.

When I began healing from depression, I became more aware of anything that lifted my mood, made me smile, relieved my upset stomach, distracted me from the stabbing pain in my chest or calmed my anxious mind.

My constant longing for any source of mental or emotional rest made me so sensitive for any kind of break or relief. I took note of these intervals and anticipated their occurrences. Then, I identified these sources of relief and held on to them. I connected the dots: the dots of depression and the dots of healing from depression. I kept the dots connected until I recovered from depression completely.

When I started learning about the direct and active role of the gut in regulating our emotional and mental conditions, the flood of information that I soaked myself in seemed like fragments of an intricate, yet very familiar puzzle. Every puzzle piece made sense.

In the next chapters I wrote all the factors that enabled me to start and complete my healing from depression. Each one of those factors is directly and indirectly related to the gut. In this chapter I want to give you some heads-up about the importance of the health of your gut, as you explore your own road to healing from depression.

There is no real chance for you to heal from depression without minding your gut and taking the time to heal it first.

Following are what present-day science tells us about our guts, as related to the mental condition of depression and chronic anxiety:

The importance of the gut lies in its "flora" and the "lining" that houses the flora:

1. Gut flora, or gut microbiota is the complex collection of trillions of microorganisms in our large intestines. These are mostly bacteria, some viruses, fungi, and protozoa.
2. The gut flora and its lining **protect us from both physical and mental illnesses**. The gut contains approximately 80% of our body's immune system cells. These cells protect us from any foreign substance we ingested with our food, water and air.
3. These immune cells are very near the vagus nerve. The vagus nerve connects our gut to our brain. **There are more neurons in the vagus nerve than in the brain**.
4. The gut bacteria and the lining of the gut are intimately connected. The gut bacteria produce the neurotransmitters, chemicals, hormones, and vitamins among others. The lining of the gut contains the neurons connecting the gut to our brain. When the efficiency of this vital communication is disturbed, the primary organ that gets affected is our brain. **Depression is one major manifestation of this disruption.**
5. **An impaired gut bacterium is directly linked to mental conditions such as anxiety, depression and autism.**

The benefits of a healthy gut:

1. A right diet and balanced gut bacteria will give us the fatty acids, amino acids, chemicals, hormones and vitamins that our body needs.

2.   Eating healthy will break unhealthy eating habits. **An unhealthy gut makes us crave for more sugar and carbohydrates.** It creates a vicious cycle of unhealthy eating lifestyle.
3.   Your body can produce more **serotonin**- the feel-good chemical that keeps us from depression. **In fact, most serotonin is produced in the gut, and only a small percentage is produced in the brain.**
4.   You will have **less mood swings**. The gut bacteria produce important brain chemicals that affect and reflect our temperament. **Any disruption in the levels of these chemicals is reflected by our mood and behavior.**
5.   A healthy gut filled with high diversity beneficial microbes will protect us from most kinds of infections, as well as carcinogenic and toxic substances. A big percentage of the stool we excrete is made up of these toxins that our good bacteria have managed to grab and neutralize. **Just like our liver, the gut's collective microbiota is a 24/7 detoxification machine.**
6.   Your body can avoid unnecessary inflammation. Ingesting processed foods will cause inflammation. **The gut, whose primary job is to extract nourishment from the food that we eat, manufacture vitamins, hormones and chemicals to make sure we're happy and unburdened by anxieties, is now left much too preoccupied with fighting inflammation.**

To promote a robust digestive health, the following are vital considerations:

1.   Normal birth gives far superior types of good bacteria than caesarian birth. The gut is initially colonized with bacteria during a normal birth - the baby swallows the microbial flora it encounters as it passes through the birth canal of the mother. **Several illnesses such as asthma, allergies and mental conditions such as depression and chronic anxieties are strongly associated with acquiring a poor set of microbes due to being deprived of a normal birth.**
2.   Breastfeeding gives babies very good microbes. Formula milk is rich in sugar that disturbs the microbiota. Soy formula delivers an even worse

blow on the baby's gut bacteria. **Being raised on formula is associated with a slew of negative health outcomes such as higher prevalence of diarrhea, ear infections, influenza, asthma, and other respiratory tract conditions, suggesting very poor immune system development.**

3. **Avoid antibiotics as much as possible.** If you really need to take antibiotics, ask your doctor if he can recommend a corresponding probiotic. Probiotics will help replenish the good bacteria in your gut.
4. **Avoid sugar and processed foods.**
5. **Minimize carbohydrates in your diet.**
6. Use healthy fats like olive oil, coconut oil, tallow, butter and lard. Avoid vegetable oils. **Consumption of these unhealthy fats will damage the lining. This is called "leaky gut".**
7. Go for high fiber diet and foods high in resistant starch. Recent studies have proven that the resulting **short-chain fatty acids** from the gut bacteria's fermentation of these resistant starch, are the best building materials for the repair of the leakiness of our gut wall. Cooked green banana has been found to have the highest concentration of resistant starch.
8. Include **fermented food** like yogurt, aged cheese, kefir, olives in brine, sauerkraut, kimchi and kombucha in your diet.

The statements above are my re-worded versions of what I have gathered from many of the most recent **science-based articles, studies and researches on the true causes of depression and anxieties.** You can find in Chapter 11 all the material support for these statements. Please do take the time to read them.

Much of these truths go against the lies that we have been made to believe about how best to care for our physical and mental health. Many of those lies have **direct and indirect effect on today's high prevalence of depression, bi-polar and anxiety disorders**. The knowledge you will derive from these readings will shatter false information you have been relying on that have contributed to your ill health, physically and mentally.

One of those many lies is the propaganda against both cholesterol and the best sources of cholesterol, the saturated fats such as coconut oil, pork fat, beef fat, chicken fat, cream, butter and eggs.

Cholesterol is an anti-inflammatory nutrient that our body utilizes 24/7 to fight inflammation. Cholesterol is also an integral component of each of our cell's membrane. Far from having the least in cholesterol quantity is the brain which has almost 25% of our body's total cholesterol, an amount not enjoyed by any other organ of the body. Cholesterol constitutes 20% of myelin, the lining that insulates, protects and regulates the functions of our nerve cells that are responsible for our thoughts, emotions and temperament.

In the same way, massive amount of cholesterol is found in our "second brain", our gut. Intestinal permeability or leaky gut, which is a major driver of inflammation, is a direct result of "cholesterol starvation". This is because the endothelial cells that line and protect our gut needs cholesterol to maintain its structural integrity.

If the body has low levels of cholesterol, we are exposing to grave impairment the very structures of both our central nervous system (the brain) and the enteric nervous system (the gut), **the two organs most responsible for our mental well-being.**

It was in the 1960s when the scientific world, with total backing of most governments and the food industry, started delivering double-knockout punches against our mental health, by:

1. Launching immense and persistent campaigns to demonize saturated fats, our body and brain's primary sources of dietary cholesterol.
2. Aggressively promoting their "proven-to-be-better" alternative to saturated fats, the highly pro-inflammatory polyunsaturated vegetable oils.

Growing up in the 70's, my health absorbed the ill effects of these two unscientific, therefore baseless dietary campaigns.

Since I was deprived of a normal, vaginal birth (I was born via caesarian section), I came into this world with weak gut microbiome. Cholesterol could have helped strengthen my gut but the formula I was fed with for all my first 8 developmental years was devoid of this healing nutrient. And then, to complete the double-jeopardy, I became addicted to fried foods cooked in vegetable oils such as canola oil and corn oil.

The damage that these foreign, manufactured, pro-inflammatory oils inflicted on my gut lining resulted to leakiness that could have been repaired by cholesterol. Unfortunately, being on a diet "low" in cholesterol rendered my immune system incapable of doing the job. This double whammy set the stage for my eventual descent into depression. I revisited this road and wrote about it in the Chapter 10 "My Long, Early and Sure Road to Depression".

All I can do is lay before you the truth about how I recovered from depression. Beyond that, I have no power to make you "see" this truth. You will have to peel off your own eyes all the lies that have covered them that prevented you from seeing the truth. However, I do suggest continuing "to stare" at these truths. Soak yourself in them. Keep educating yourself. And soon enough those scales of lies will fall off and these walls of truth can take over to guard you and your health.

PRACTICAL GUIDE:
1. Watch this <u>video:</u> Australian Saturated Fat & Cholesterol Documentary:
   https://www.youtube.com/watch?v=1pfGTBXkq3g&t=640s
2. Sugar and vegetable oils (hydrogenated and liquid, including margarine) are **two of the most inflammatory substances** that harm our gut lining and microbes. (Not to mention the damage they do to our

arteries. Both substances have been proven by reliable scientific studies to be the primary cause of arterial damage. And yet, cholesterol, who comes to "repair" the damage, is the one blamed for these arterial plaques. *"Blaming heart disease on cholesterol is like blaming a fire on the firemen who arrive to put out the flames."* as so aptly put by Ms. Sally Fallon-Morrell, in her article with Ms. Mary G. Enig, "It's The Beef" *D.3.1)*.

Vegetable oils are in almost everything "processed" that we eat: canned foods, breads, sodas, crackers, chips, and even salad dressings that are made with unstable oils such as corn oil, soybean oil, canola oil, safflower oil, sunflower oil, peanut oil, and cottonseed oil. **Hence, the first way you can avoid these gut-insulting substances is to eat home-prepared food as often as you can, most especially your main meals. This way you can control the ingredients that go in your food: you can make them healthy and delicious at the same time.**

If you're out in a restaurant having a salad bowl full of the best organic greens BUT smothered with a dressing made with part olive oil and part unnatural vegetable oil, then you are not giving your gut the best chance to extract the nutrients from these greens. The bugs in your gut would most probably be preoccupied in making sure that the inflammation that will arise from the presence of this foreign substance (vegetable oil) is kept under control.

So, the big question is "What is the right oil to use for cooking?". Here in my kitchen, we have been using **beef tallow** D.3.5) since 2013. We use this healthy fat in almost every cooking that requires oil: light frying, deep frying and sautéing. Another fat we use is good quality real butter. Butter is usually what we use in frying eggs. But when we fry bacon, we then use the bacon drippings to fry in our eggs or anything else that can absorb the fat.

My point is: you should not rely on other people to care for the health of your gut, and in turn your mental health. A non-inflammatory, healing diet is your quickest, best chance to reverse whatever ill state your gut is in right now. It's our most powerful tool because it's the most effective. And it's a tool you can easily manipulate and which, believe it or not, you have the instinct to execute.

3. **Avoid processed sugar and foods high in carbohydrates.** Carbohydrates is the only macronutrient that we least need to get through diet. It is because our body can make it on its own whenever there's deficiency in carbs. If there is one biggest lever that had propelled us towards very poor mental health, it is our reliance on the food pyramid that urged us to allot the biggest portion of our calories through carbohydrates.

You need to switch those pyramid labels and assign the biggest bulk of your daily calories for natural fats and fibers, and the tip and smallest allotment for carbohydrates and "natural, not processed" sweeteners like honey and maple syrup.

Just remember that fatty foods like fatty cuts of beef and pork, and butter and cream are nutrient and calorie-dense, which means that a small amount goes a long way. It means you need not consume as much fats as you used to. However, there's a big "UNLESS" that follows. And it's UNLESS you want to eat as much butter and as much steaks and as much pork chops as you used to. If that's how you feel like doing, then go ahead and do it. Just remember that you have "reversed" the labels. Meaning, you cannot eat a lot of fats and a lot of carbohydrates at the same time.

Let go of the carbohydrates, and then you can embrace as much fats and fibers as you want.

4. When you avoid sugary foods and foods cooked in and with vegetable oils, it will turn down the level of inflammation in your gut. **Eating more natural fats and fiber will provide your gut the raw materials to repair and rebuild the gut lining and help seal the leaks.** The soluble kind of fiber will provide some level of nutrition for the gut bacteria themselves. **But what will boost the diversity of your gut microbiota, provide immense source energy for the gut bacteria and tip the scale in their favor is a consistent supply of fermented foods.**

   Try to research your own culture's fermented foods. The Japanese love natto, which is a fermented soybean food. Korean cuisine is rich in kimchi, a spicy and delicious fermented cabbage dish. Germany introduced us to another kind of fermented cabbage, sauerkraut. Here in the Philippines, as in many of our Asian neighbors, we are fond of fermented fish and shrimp sauces, which we can incorporate in many of our dishes.

   Other fermented foods universally available are yoghurt and yoghurt drinks, bitter chocolates, coffee, kombucha, and kefir.

These days I regard my gut as like a bank account. I keep it well-funded as I know I might need to withdraw from it when "needy and demanding" stress comes knocking.

Some days, I regard it like an HR department - I try to keep it as diversified as possible but of the highest standard, because once again, I need to be able to tap it for anyone that the rest of my body's departments might need at any given day (not the least of which is the "Fire Department of Inflammations").

I am not yet the richest or the expert in so far as the health of my gut is concerned. But I have made good progress. I still have physical conditions which tell and remind me that I can't ignore my gut bugs too long a time. However, I no longer suffer from depression and intense anxieties.

How I arrived from "there to here": from a bankrupt gut to a funded one; from a lonesome HR to a thriving and diverse one; how I completed my healing from depression and intense anxieties, all the details I had laid out in the next chapters.

I implore you to be patient. Eat some yoghurt, take a couple of flush-free niacin (Vitamin B3; I'll tell you more about this) and try to avoid sugars and vegetable oils for the next couple of days.

Gear up as I guide you out of your pit of depression.

CHAPTER 3: UNDERSTAND THE TRIGGERS

The two main reasons that triggered the start of my depression and severe anxieties were:

1. Poor health; and
2. Mammoth-size stresses due to bad decisions

THE FIRST TRIGGER: Poor Health

I was not aware of the first reason – that I was unhealthy. I only knew I had hypo or under-active thyroid. I've had this since my early teens. Other than that, I thought I was healthy since I played badminton aggressively and went to the gym regularly. That was my whole basis for health. I didn't see the importance of taking any vitamins or supplements and my diet composed mainly of fast foods and sugary stuff.

Prior to my depression, I never had any major illness and I felt strong physically. I was concerned about "nutritional deficiency" as far as my two young boys were concerned but never for me. I didn't know then how nutritional deficiencies, compromised gut health, toxicity, and hormonal imbalance can play major roles with our temper and basic emotions. I had no clue that these conditions can make or break one's ability to handle stress.

According to my extensive research on depression, if at the time a person faces a severe source of stress, her body's nutritional and gut health condition, toxicity and hormone levels are out of whack, she will most likely succumb to depression and anxiety attacks.

Today, I now understand what triggered my depression and intense anxieties. **My deficient diet, imbalanced hormones, toxic lifestyle and weak thyroid were the perfect setting for an emotional and psychological catastrophe. My body was weak. My defenses were down. And then the stresses depleted whatever physiological reserves I had.**

By the time I had to make those crucial business decisions, I gravitated towards impulsiveness, with little regard or study about the consequences. My mental and physical health simply could not support me to make the right decisions.

Unfortunately, since my husband was still working abroad, I had to face the repercussions of my actions and decisions head-on, alone. I had no time to relax or gear-up. The aftermath was immediate and intense. My coping mechanisms started to break under the pressure of having no alternative but to keep on going.

It was only after a matter of weeks - when the first signs of depression started to manifest. I experienced muscle and hand jitters that worsened to weakness of knees and other joints. My insomnia soon led to painful palpitations. The palpitations became agonizing chest sensations that felt like a knife perpetually stuck into my chest. My mind was in a constant state of panic and I walked like a zombie during the day.

I implied in the Introduction that I don't believe that stress is one of the **causes** of depression.

I don't.

I believe that the body, in an ideal state of health, should be able to deal with various kinds and levels of stresses, without surrendering to depression.

A few months ago, my housekeeper approached me. She was crying and shaking. As she sobbed, she explained that her husband, who was in the province, had an accident at work. He crushed a finger of his right hand as it caught in a mechanical equipment. Immediately, I gave her 3 capsules of flush-free Niacin. Within 20 minutes, she was calm, and the shaking had stopped.

I explained to her how Niacin or Vitamin B3 works in the gut (then brain) by enabling us to think clearly and see the problem for what it is. Nothing more than its true size. After 30 minutes, in a much calmer manner she said that her husband's employer will shoulder all the medical expenses and he should be able to go back to work in a couple of weeks. I asked her if she had known this even before she told me the news. She said yes. I asked her if there was anything else that worried her. She said she's not worried anymore. Just like that in less than an hour.

I told her to stop drinking soda and to avoid sweet foods, both of which she was fond of. I explained to her how sugar steals the nutrients we get from food and how it harms the lining of our gut. I explained how a leaky gut can affect how we handle stress and how we view problems. During that period, we constantly had bone broth and I told her to take bone broth more frequently. She promptly complied.

After a couple weeks she was happy to see she's lost some weight, and her stomach acidity and tendencies to panic had gone. Without the constant assault of sugar, the inflammation in her gut was doused. It had time to shift gears and start repair on its leakiness. The cholesterol and gelatin provided by the bone broth were the needed materials for this repair.

Then just a couple weeks ago, she received news that her son was rushed to the hospital for constant vomiting and that she needed an advance from her salary. She broke to me this news in a way that was so different from months back when she told me about her husband. She was still visibly worried, but she stood upright. Though her eyes were red, her general demeanor was calm. Again, I gave her Niacin but this time, it is the better state of her gut that carried her through and allowed her to stay calm despite the presence of a severe stress.

THE SECOND TRIGGER: Mammoth-size stresses due to bad decisions

The most that we should categorize "stress" under is being a **trigger**, not the cause. A person may either be so affected by a source of stress or not at all. It all depends on the state of his shield: HIS GUT.

For as long as we are alive in this world, we will experience stress. **To try to avoid stress is in fact an impractical way to avoid depression**. Our job is to make sure we are prepared for them, WHEN they come. Our shield must be up and strong, WHEN stresses come.

I capitalized "when" for two reasons. I entered depression because: my health was weak and because the stresses that came had added weight because they were my own doing.

LET STRESS COME. DON'T INVITE IT.

Let me explain by giving an analogy.

In the wild, where all sorts of dangers abound, a man and his family build a home. They gather the materials they will need in building both the house itself and the perimeter fence that will provide protection for the whole property and the family. Their knowledge of the kinds of perils in the area will guide them not only in choosing the materials but also the techniques to use in building their property's wall of defense.

Knowing all too well that they are only as safe as the integrity of their defensive wall, they put everything they've got to making sure it is of utmost quality and strength. For example, they will make sure that this wall of defense can withstand a sudden attack by a pack of wolves, or a group of lions or even a band of savages with their weapons of destruction.

Only after the man and his family have done their due diligence, with the wall of defenses up and sturdy, can they finally rest. They can relax inside the property and enjoy life knowing that they are well protected.

What this family DOES NOT do is go out of the property to seek out these dangers and provoke them to test their defense's integrity. They don't try to taunt the lions into anger to get them to attack the property. They don't purposely offend their savage neighbors and stir them to anger. They don't instigate a conflict. They don't invite danger, unnecessarily.

The paragraph above may initially seem ludicrous to you. Who does that, right? Who wants danger to come knocking at our door? No one.

But the truth is, unknowingly, that is exactly what we do when we fail to follow the proper roadmap for life. What you see in a such a life are discontent, strife, anger, frustration and much unhappiness. **These are the wolves of stresses that we have inadvertently invited to come and weaken our physiological health: our Number 1 wall of defense against depression.**

To start with, I didn't have the required health that I needed. Worse, I attracted those stresses towards me through the wrong decisions I made. I made things even worse by trying to solve the problems with pride and arrogance.

IT IS THE WHOLE YOU

I realized that I neglected not just the health of my body but also that of my soul.

I had mentioned in the Introduction of this book that, throughout the entire period of my depression, I had never taken an anti-depressant pill because I didn't have any budget for any kind of treatment or medications.

The second reason that I didn't mention is this: deep in my heart and mind, I was sure that only God could show me the path to healing.

I knew this for certain because I could feel the thick space that disconnected me from God. And that thick space was full of me, mine and myself. I could no longer feel that sweet fellowship with God I used to enjoy. He was there, at a distance. He never left me. But I had strayed away. When He prodded me to go right, I went left. When He whispered about the longer but surer way, I chose the shortest, quickest route. When He reminded me that it was better to exercise patience, understanding and forgiveness, I insisted on being vengeful and expressing hate.

I chose and took the steps that got me to where I was.

I had known and was familiar with the practicality of the Bible. For me it wasn't only a spiritual Book. **It was my life's road map**. I knew that what I needed to do was to look at and re-study the Road Map, the Word of God. It was my way back. It would surely show me the way out of my messes.

As I started to re-study the Word of God, it showed me the areas of my life that needed examination and re-alignment. As the text of the Bible shone its light on these areas, it was a constant emotional rollercoaster ride: extreme highs and lows. Most days I wasn't a willing and compliant student. Most times I refused to accept that I had made that mistake or this mistake, and so forth, and those days were dark and heavy. I wrestled with the truths in the Word of God. But I plodded on and on, letting myself be broken open and exposed to God by His Word.

How the Lord healed my soul is what the second book in this series is all about. In it I wrote about all the areas in my life and personality that God put His finger on, and the most gracious ways He dealt with each one.

PRACTICAL GUIDE

Take No-Flush Niacin with a buffered or non-acidic Vitamin C. If you prefer the regular Vitamin C, then take it with some food. My daily maintenance is 2 capsules Niacin (500 mg each) and 1 capsule 1,000 mg regular Vitamin C. I double my niacin dosage on those days I am sure to face more stresses. Take also very high-quality fish oil or better yet, a high-quality cod-liver oil. It will help nourish your brain and repair the damaged cells.

* * *

Addressing the condition of your physiological health - your **body** - will pull you out of depression. It is like having a house with its defenses intact and strong. The principles of healing that I wrote about in this book, if promptly acted upon, will cause you to see which way "UP" is. And then it will enable you to swiftly rise out of your pit of depression

Once out of depression, there's always the possibility of falling back in, when we unwisely invite stresses through the foolish ways we conduct our life's affairs.

Addressing the health of your **soul and spirit** will keep depression miles away. Stresses will still come. But you will deal with them, unburdened by any guilt of being responsible for them.

---

3 John 2 The Voice (VOICE)
My beloved friend, I pray that everything is going well for you and that your body is as healthy as your soul is prosperous.

CHAPTER 4: ACCEPT AND EMBRACE THE NECESSARY PERIOD OF INFLAMMATION

My researches tell me that, right after any type of injury, the factors the body needs to start the process of inflammation are already existing in the body, ready to jump for action.

Our body is equipped to contain an injury and initiate the healing process. Inflammation is our body's emergency response team. It's our 911. That's the reason why any invasive wound, like cuts or punctures, swell within minutes.

The same thing happens when you sprain your ankle. When you overstretch your muscles and ligaments, many of the muscle strands break and tear. In 10 to 20 minutes, that area will swell up, redden, feel hotter than the rest of the surrounding areas. And then it will throb with pain for the next several hours or even days.

This whole process of inflammation is the body's attempt to contain the injury, to make sure it doesn't spread and that it is not provoked any further.

PRACTICAL GUIDE:

From here on forward, you need to regard your depression as something that carries a purpose. Ask yourself these questions:

1. Where am I now?
2. Where was I before I started feeling this way?
3. What was it that I was doing (activity, food, environment)?

A few months after I healed from depression, I bumped into a friend at the supermarket. He asked me why I stopped playing badminton. With some hesitation I told him about my depression. After a few minutes, I noticed he was staring at me, but his mind was obviously somewhere else. Then he said "My goodness! I didn't know that I've been suffering from depression." He told me all about his symptoms - almost exactly what I had: weakness of knees and arms, constant palpitations, extreme pessimism, feelings of foreboding, insomnia and inability to feel joy or happiness. At that time though, he was right in the middle of it.

During this time, I had just started my researches on depression and its root causes. I had just read some research papers on how a high-sugar diet can inflict such damage on the lining of our gut. And how this can lead to inflammation, and eventually be a big contributing factor why people fall into depression. I told him that he might think of himself as very unqualified to fall into depression. He was a happily married man. He worked as an executive in a huge corporation. He was active and generally well-liked in our village. And then I told him about my researches.

And then I asked him if he suspected anything that might have triggered his depression. He said he remembered that the very first time he felt unusually jittery was the morning after a long night of heavy coffee drinking. The coffee he was drinking was the 3 in 1 kind that's rich in processed sugar. He said he was never the same after that. The jitters never left, but instead intensified into muscle weakness.

He worked in a company that manufactured coffee mixes, sugared drinks and his family had a constant supply of this gut-inflammatory beverages. At that point, I didn't even feel the need to ask to him to stop drinking instant coffee mixes and sodas. He was already staring at the face of the main trigger of his depression.

Depression was showing him how he was harming his body.

✳ ✳ ✳

Just like with my friend, depression set in to immobilize me. My body knew exactly what to use to call my attention. It needed me to stop attracting stresses towards me. It needed me to slow down because I was just running on nutritional dregs. It needed to recharge, to heal and repair itself.

DEPRESSION is our body's way of preserving itself - to give it time to do nothing else other than prepare for the next process which is HEALING.

During this period, just when the swelling subsides, the actual healing starts. And the milestone that kick-started my "physical" healing was the day I was overcome by an **intense craving for the sun.**

It was Day One of my healing from depression.

CHAPTER 5: GET REACQUAINTED WITH YOUR NORTH STAR

I WAS NOT "LOSING" IT

It was right after my day's Bible meditation. I realized I was staring at the rays of the morning sun reflected at the wall adjacent to the window. Suddenly, I felt the sun's rays hot on my skin and I saw myself walking with my face lifted towards the sun. I blinked and realized I was imagining everything! I had goosebumps because I "felt" the hot sun boring into my skin. I asked myself "what just happened?"

I was never a sun-lover. I loved the rain, and when it's gloomy and downcast and the streets are wet…that's what I loved. I never liked walking out in the sun and the dry dusty streets. Uh-uh. That isn't me, I thought, and so I brushed this "sun-cravings "aside.

The next morning, the craving was back and in stronger intensity. Once again, I imagined myself walking under the hot morning sun, from the front of the house all the way to the farthest phase of our village. However, my dread for any outside social interactions got the better of me each time I was about to put on my rubber shoes. Hence, it took me many days before I finally gave in to these sun cravings.

When the day finally came, as soon as I finished tying my rubber shoes' laces, I felt a sense of courage rising within me. I told myself "Rose you don't have to engage in a fake, friendly conversation, but you can manage to be polite and maybe a smile". So, at 8:15am, I stepped out onto our street and headed towards the inner, farther part of the village.

After 15 minutes, my knees felt weaker than ever and I started to regret the decision to leave the safety of our house. Five more minutes later, the sun broke out and my face instinctively lifted towards the sun. I remember slowing down my already slow pace because I had closed my eyes and held my face in the sunshine. I couldn't remember how long. It was the first time in months that I felt something physically pleasant and enjoyable.

For the past seven or eight months, I felt this relief only in my soul and my spirit whenever I was reading and meditating on the Word of God. Sensing it on my skin, on my physical being, was making me ecstatic with joy! I wanted to jump up and down right there in the middle of the street. Instead, I let that surge of energy fuel my walking speed. What started as wobbly and tentative steps a few minutes ago became brisk and determined.

I reached the farthest part of the village where the street ended with the gate of the neighboring factory. I touched that gate and turned back home.

On my walk back, I felt the same hot pleasing sensation on the back of my neck and I exposed my neck more by pulling down the neckline of my sweater. Fifteen more minutes later I reached home, and I was drenched with warm sweat. For the first time since we transferred to that house, I climbed the stairs in double steps, barely holding on to the handles. The next 4 to 5 hours were the most energetic I have felt in months. Though the anxieties were back in full force as the evening neared, that day marked the very first time that I felt excited for the next day.

KEEPING AT IT

I brisk-walked at least 4 mornings each week from 8:30 to 9:30. I kept at this until the rainy season came. In the beginning, I always had my sweater's hood and sunglasses on and removed them when I reached the street where the houses were few and far between. One time I heard my name called by an acquaintance and I realized I had started walking without my hood and sunglasses on and so my face was completely exposed. I waved and smiled but I couldn't voice out any greeting, so I just kept walking. The joy I was feeling was too important to get deterred by any fear for social interaction.

The physical healing that followed my daily exposure to the sun was tremendous. About the 3rd month since I started my morning walks, I realized that my knees were no longer wobbly. I no longer need to stay by the walls when I walk around the house.

As my knees and joints improved, my emotional and psychological conditions improved. I felt less and less anxious or worried about our problems. The problems didn't disappear. But I could see them clearly for what they were and for the size they were. There was no multiplying effect anymore. The anxieties that used to magnify these problems and made them seem much bigger than they were, soon evaporated. I was able to look at the problems in the face, measure them their true size and plan my strategies in solving them.

Nearing the end of my 2nd year of depression, my two-a.m. automatic wake-up time became 3am then 4am then 5am. However, the painful knife-in-the-chest sensation remained, though with lessening intensity, until almost the very end of my depression.

WHATS WITH THE SUN AND DEPRESSION?

The healing that I felt through exposure to the sun felt like I was doused in liquid revitalizing light that penetrated my aching muscles, bones and joints. The immediate, resulting manifestation was energy and strength in my extremities, hips, back and neck. This translated to swifter movements, very much unlike the tentative, painful stride I barely managed to do for many months.

How the sun can do all those miraculous changes in the body has a lot to do with how vitamin D works synergistically with vitamins A, E, K2 and other crucial minerals like Calcium, Magnesium and Zinc. When all these nutrients are present in the body, the repair and healing can be done wherever they are needed.

In the absence of proper nutritious foods, what provided me the other needed components to work with Vitamin D, were the multi-vitamins my sister sent to me in bulk from the US. I had been taking these supplements since about the time my depression started.

I could imagine all these vitamins and minerals, fully-geared up and patiently waiting for the arrival of vitamin D. There must have been great celebration in my body as soon as Vitamin D arrived and was excitedly welcomed by the waiting "healing crew", because that was exactly how I felt: **happiness and excitement over things I couldn't even figure out yet at the time.**

The following benefits are known and proven to be associated with sun exposure therapy. Each one of these benefits, in one way or another, played vital roles in my initial healing from depression:

1. Sun exposure helps our gut produce more serotonin (nature's anti-depressant) which then helps to lift our mood. I felt this change in me within the first hour of being exposed to the sun. Once again, I knew what happiness felt!
2. Sun exposure improves brain function, by increasing the neurotransmitters endorphins. Together with the work done by serotonin and dopamine, they help the brain have stability when

dealing with the stresses of life. It calmed me down and I noticed much less impulsiveness in my thoughts, reactions and actions.

3. Sun exposure facilitates the production and release of vitamin D3 which helps our bones absorb calcium which then improves bone health. With the help of vitamins, A and K2, vitamin D helps in making sure that our arteries do not develop calcification that can lead to heart ailments. Although that pain in my chest didn't completely disappear until the end of the 3rd year of my depression, its diminishing intensity was very noticeable.

4. Sun exposure enables the discharge of nitric oxide which then helps normalize blood pressure. These nitric oxides are just right under the skin, waiting to be hit by the sun's rays, like soldiers ready for action. The symptoms of high blood pressure are: fatigue, chest pain, difficulty breathing, irregular heartbeat, pounding in the chest, neck, or ears. All these symptoms, except for chest pain, gradually diminished within the first 8 to 10 months after I started my heliotherapy. The chest pains completely disappeared by the end of the 3rd year, which marked my exit from the pit of my depression.

5. Sun exposure sends appropriate signals to the pineal gland with instructions on when and how much melatonin to produce and thus improves sleep quality. Within days of being exposed to the sun, my sleep patterns and quality gradually improved.

PRACTICAL GUIDE:

No matter how you got into your depression pit, you need the sunshine vitamin to help your body heal and repair. Choose the time when the sun's rays are in their most vertical (10 am to 3 pm). All you need is 10 minutes of direct sun exposure on one area. Not through a glass partition. It must be direct on your skin. Apply sunscreen on your face, neck and nape. Most often, I exposed my entire legs and my back. You don't have to expose all or most of your skin. **Your entire body will benefit from the sun even when you expose only a portion of it**. However, for skin diseases like eczema and psoriasis, it is best to expose the affected skin itself. Sun bathing my back also relieved my lungs from asthma.

If your situation and location do not permit you to have sun exposure, then take vitamin D3 supplements, along with vitamins A and K2. There are benefits from sun exposure that cannot be replaced with vitamin supplementation. However, that should not stop you from getting whatever you can from other sources like supplementation and nutritious, natural foods.

Various internet sources give differing half-life period for vitamin D3. Some say 5 days, others say 15 days. What I get from this is that, daily exposure to the sun is not necessary to maintain enough vitamin D levels. Same with supplementation. However, in my case, having lost my parathyroid from my total-thyroidectomy surgery, I must take high calcium dosage daily, to prevent osteoporosis. As a result, I do need daily doses of vitamin D and K2 to make sure that the calcium goes to where they should go, which is my bones, and not my arteries.

As I reached this part of the chapter, I pondered how to best end it. I heard my husband call out my name and asked me if I wanted to watch something from Netflix. I reluctantly removed my fingers from the keyboard and joined my husband to choose something from Netflix's available selection. He wanted to start watching the series Planet Earth. I agreed, half-heartedly. But within the first twenty minutes of watching the first episode "From Pole to Pole", I was enveloped with inspiration.

Mr. David Attenborough, the narrator said, **"All animals, rare or common, ultimately depend for their energy on the sun."** This is true for almost all living things.

In the sun, my body found its True North. Just as an elephant knows where to go and how to replenish its body's depleting supply of sodium to stay alive; just as the chimpanzees know how to get rid of their intestinal parasitic worms by eating hundreds of leaves toxic to these parasites; just as parrots peck on hills of clay to flush out poisons from their guts; just as the female emperor penguin knows that she is not strong enough for the task, she then entrusts her egg to her male partner for the difficult and long period of incubation; just as dogs and cats eat grass to induce vomiting in their efforts to rid their guts of toxins; and just as a sea turtle, after so many years and thousands of miles of being away, return to the very beach upon which it was hatched; **I knew, when my face instinctively lifted towards the sun, which I never before this time appreciated, that it was what I needed to start my body's process of healing from depression.**

CHAPTER 6: GIVE IN TO YOUR BODY'S TRUE CRAVINGS

A few months after I started my daily morning brisk walks, I began to feel strong cravings for **fresh milk: the raw, unpasteurized kind (E.1)** that I used to drink as a young girl. Back then, I remember the happiness I felt each time a cousin would arrive from the province carrying with her bottles of fresh raw cow or carabao milk. Not even the most expensive powdered or pasteurized milk can come close to the creaminess and deliciousness of fresh raw milk.

Unfortunately, at that time of my depression, since I had no access nor the budget for raw milk, I pushed these cravings aside. But the cravings persisted. And as it intensified, these milk cravings alternated with cravings for juicy, fatty burger patties, for thick fatty slices of beef, then much later on for **salmon (F.1)**, coconut meat and even **chicken feet (H.5)**. These strong and specific food cravings started around the middle of my third year of being depressed and gradually increased in intensity way after my depression.

By this time, I had been meditating on the Word of God for more than two years, doing my morning brisk walks for more than a year, but still eating the same type of low nutrient cheap foods. However, I had started to receive huge bottles of supplements from my sister who had emigrated to the U.S., which turned out to be one of my saving graces, in the absence of daily nutritious foods.

REALIZE THAT HEALING NECESSITATES REPAIR

When my body shifted from inflammation to healing and repair, it activated my cravings for the sun, and for all the rest of the materials needed for repair, which my body realized it didn't have enough of: vitamins D, C, A, and E, Calcium, Magnesium, K2, Zinc, the amino acids, B vitamins, and so on. From my researches, I found out the specific nutrients that the foods I was craving for could offer and how these nutrients directly help a person recover from emotional and psychological conditions like depression and anxiety, and physical manifestations like joint and muscle weakness, palpitations and chest pains.

Please note I did these researches after the fact, a couple of years after the end of the most severe period of my depression. My depression period was from end of 2007 to end of 2010. I started my online research on depression and anxiety around middle of 2012. When I learned about the nutrients these foods I was craving for could offer, I immediately allotted a monthly budget for them. I did so because of one main thing: **the cravings have never left me even when I knew I was out of the pit of depression already.**

Also, even when I was "out" of the pit, occasionally, I still felt being enveloped by the "memories" of it and I showed symptoms of being depressed, like being jittery, and palpitations. I was out of depression, but it felt like trying to fly away and yet one foot was kept tethered in the pit.

MORE SEEMINGLY IRRATIONAL CRAVINGS

I was in one of these depression "memory days", when I had a dream, sometime in the middle of 2012 about salmon. In the dream, I was standing in front of our kitchen sink staring at 2 huge live salmon fish as they swam around in the kitchen sink. They could hardly fit in the sink and water was getting splashed over on the counter. I woke up salivating for the taste of salmon and within hours I was at the supermarket buying several kilos of salmon head, the cheapest parts.

Two hours later I was feasting on my **Sinigang na Salmon sa Miso (F.7),** a variant of a Filipino dish made with sour soup from tamarind. I felt so satisfied and peculiarly happy. That evening I found myself looking up online what it was with Salmon and if there was any connection with what I felt a few hours after eating it, which was a weird sense of elation.

I was so surprised by the wealth of information available online. This is the beginning of my researches about food cravings. After researching on the benefits of salmon, I then researched about benefits of **beef fats, tendons and bone marrow (D.3.1), pork fats, chicken feet/skin, "balut" (D.1.10),** coconut meat **(I.1)** , beef liver **(A.2.14)** and raw, unpasteurized milk **(E.4).**

Alternating with long periods of cravings for these healthy fatty foods were short "bursts" of cravings for my favorite vegetables and fruits, like *talbos ng kamote* **(sweet potato tops) (N.1),** our native *petchay* **(a type of cabbage),** *kangkong* **(water spinach)(N.3), apples and mangos, and avocados (L.1).**

My cravings for avocados started 2008 but left ignored until 2013. I ignored them most probably because they were mild cravings, sort of like a much quieter whisper than those by beef fat and chicken feet. Apples and mangoes were my favorite fruits when I was little. Strong cravings for these came back during my depression. But this time, for apples, I wanted to eat only the skin and the flesh right under. I find the taste of it very pleasurable and didn't feel the same satisfaction when eating the rest of the flesh.

Also, it is worth noting that I had experienced strong cravings for certain foods even before the onset of my depression. One strong craving was for **squash and watermelon seeds (P.1)**. In 2006, just over a year before I entered depression, I remember eating bags of these at least 3 to 4 consecutive days. I bought the ones still with the seed husks on and I would end up with bowls full of the opened husks. Sometimes I would wait until I had opened lots of seeds and then pop a palm full in my mouth. The pleasure I felt as the seeds turn to mush in my mouth was intense which drove me to open more seeds.

In Chapter 8, I have included the results of my researches on the benefits derived from eating these foods in relation to my conditions at the time of my cravings.

PRACTICAL GUIDE:

1. In a notebook, list down everything your body and emotions have been manifesting ever since you started your depression (anxieties, negative thoughts, anger or rage, weakness in joints and muscles, any pain areas, insomnia, etc.) Then make another list of all the cravings you've been experiencing (for example: butter, eggs, bacon, fish, nature, sun).

    Research online about the nutrients that these items can provide to help you heal from your depression symptoms. There is no way around this task. You must do your due diligence.

    Just like its Maker, the body is intelligent. It knows when it's sick and it sends signals that give clues on what it needs to heal and repair itself. After making your lists, analyze which of these cravings can you respond to right away and act on them.

2. If you have been on anti-depressants, consult your doctor on how you can be appropriately weaned out of it. Do not be surprised if your doctor "refuse" to wean you out of anti-depressants. Unless your doctor appreciates some background on naturopathy, it is very unlikely

that he would welcome an intervention that doesn't include anti-depressants.

If he proves to be close-minded and refuse to try to take you off these pills, then do some research to find a naturopathic doctor in your area. Should you find one, never ever again take their word at face value, without double or triple checking their recommendations against various available data on their safeness and efficacy, which you can do online. Do not completely entrust your health into the hands of one person, no matter how credible and well-meaning he may seem. Take an active part in your health. No one can ever care enough for your body than the person it belongs to: you.

I have read articles written by survivors of depression who, after being on anti-depressants for many years without marked and stable improvements, shifted to natural methods of healing such as vitamin supplementations and healthy, natural, and organic foods. All of them were weaned out of anti-depressants in a gradual manner, during the shift to supplementation and eating healthy. If you cannot locate a naturopathic doctor who can guide you at this stage, then you must double your efforts in educating yourself on the safest and proven ways to be weaned out.

Whatever you do, do not stop your anti-depressants abruptly.

3. Take no-flush Niacin (Vitamin B3)$_B$ as often as you need, always with vitamin C.

SAMPLE CASE 1: My brother-in-law had recently gone through a very trying emotional and psychological set back. He started to feel jittery, alternating from being non-communicative to talking with much anxiety, and having insomnia. He went to a psychiatrist for consult. As expected, the psychiatrist prescribed anti-depressants. He was at the pharmacy, about to buy the pills, when my sister remembered what I've repeatedly babbled about with regards to Niacin's wondrous ability in providing emotional and psychological stability. He decided to first try his chances on Niacin. The relief he felt was almost immediate: an hour or less after taking his first capsules. Within days of taking no-flush niacin with vitamin C, he was back with his usual animated way of expressing himself. Most importantly, he could finally look at the source of his anxieties, with the needed calmness of mind and heart, and was soon analyzing his plan of action to solve the problem.

I would like to theorize that my brother-in-law quickly responded to niacin and bounced back in a matter of days because everything else was intact in him. He is physically fit. He walks almost daily with my sister under the hot sun of Reno, Nevada. My sister always made sure that she served the family nutritious home-cooked food. Her voice was one I had constantly heard, from way back in my childhood, always pushing us her siblings to eat natural, unprocessed food. She also despised the effects of antibiotics in the body and over the years kept her sentinel role against it for her husband and kids.

This refusal to take anti-biotics alone played a huge role in keeping my brother-in-law's gut healthy.

On the spiritual side, his whole family attends church on a weekly basis, sometimes even twice a week. They have a happy, supportive and contented family life, enjoying all their grandkids and the arrival of a new granddaughter.

This ideal scenario did not immune him from the effects of the stresses that came. But these very factors that made up his overall health are what kept him from completely losing his equilibrium. **When that trying circumstance came, all it could do was tip the scale slightly and it was swiftly and promptly corrected by Niacin. This just shows how our body, given the right physiological balance and harmony we call "homeostasis", can thrive and prosper under the most trying life events.**

SAMPLE CASE 2: Unfortunately, for the other case example I know, this young patient's hellish journey through manic depression is stubbornly rooted into malnourishment that started from his infant years and has remained unchanged to this very day.

Upon my relentless prodding, the parents incorporated supplementation including high dosage of niacin and vitamin C. On occasions, these two vitamins had broken through the thick fog of his bipolar condition. However, the patient's daily diet remains the same: unrestrained high carbohydrates meals and an almost total absence of greens and other vegetables.

Vitamin supplementation is simply not enough to arrest and heal the patient's gut dysbiosis which has manipulated his mind and behavior. What makes his situation worse is that he sees at least 3 psychiatrists and each one, at the first stages of treatment had expressed mild to zero interest over what proper diet and supplementations can do to mental health. Only when their patient had exhausted all their recommendations and now much sicker than when he first started did they start pushing the parents to "care for the child's gut".

The following are the changes I have repeatedly observed in my mental, physical and emotional condition a few minutes after taking niacin:

a. I feel neither excited nor inhibited. I feel stable. My physical reactions accurately reflect how I feel: not jumpy, voice doesn't crack, can talk with confidence and my eyes don't dart here and there as they do when I feel nervous.
b. My heartbeats are quieter; I don't need to breathe deeply (thus, visibly) often.
c. Since my experience with depression, my appetite for social interactions had diminished. I developed anxiety when interacting with members of the "upper class". Part of the ritual of meeting someone

new is having to shake their hands which I try to avoid because my palm would be sweaty, cold and jittery. But on niacin, all these are gone. In place of anxiety is confidence; I offer my hand at the same time the person does; and my hand is almost always warm, unless I'm in a very cold room. I don't shy away from small talk anymore. I still don't initiate them, unless it's necessary that I do so.

d. On niacin, I focus more in finding solutions to problems. This doesn't mean that I always manage to promptly come up with solutions. But that period between problems and solutions has become a much quieter and less stressful time for me. I can now sleep peacefully even with an unsolved problem or a source of worry lurking behind.

It's very important to purposely notice these changes - to distinguish darkness from light and acknowledge it. Doing so would make you remember to be vigilant with taking these supplements, thus helping you be more responsible for your own well-being.

4. Avoid anything that will further harm your gut microbiota. Have more of what can promote its health. Make a list of all the changes that you can manage to do right now.

Do not focus on things that are out of reach for the moment. For example, I didn't despair when I couldn't respond to my raw milk cravings and other foods that were then beyond my budget. However, having read about the "emptiness" of processed sugars, and how they steal nutrients from being available for absorption by my body's cells, I gradually and steadily lessened the presence of processed sugar in my diet.

The items that I initially eliminated were the following:

a. instant coffee mixes – the 3-in-1 kinds that Filipinos are so fond of. I now brew my coffee and add coconut sugar and heavy cream and real butter.

b. Breakfast cereals – I used to add honey to further sweeten the milk the "natural" way. I found out that the honey I used was mainly syrup fillers. These days, I still give in to my rare "false craving" for cereal. But I now add raw milk and I chew very slowly. It's amazing how pleasure is multiplied just by chewing your food more consciously. It helps avoid urges eat more from feeling of not having eaten enough.

c. hot chocolate mixes – I'm still into hot chocolate but now I make my own using high quality pure cacao, coconut sugar and heavy cream.

d. chewing gums – I was a gum-chain-eater and would spit out the gum as soon as the sweetness has gone and pop in a new one. I replaced them with sugar-free gums which I seldom indulge in.

e. sugared water and sodas – these are major anti-nutrient substances. Get them out of your pantry as soon as you can. You will have to learn to appreciate drinking plain water. And the best and fastest way to increase your appreciation of plain water is to drink MORE of it. Turn to cold water even when you are most thirsty and pay attention to how quickly it has relieved your thirst. You will have to constantly give your mind chances to replace its ingrained wrong perceptions of food with truths.

f. Also, I eliminated the use of **vegetable oils (D.2)** in cooking. As previously noted, vegetable oils, such as canola and corn oil, have been proven to be one of the major (or THE major) causes of arterial and so many other kinds of inflammation. It was several more months before I learned about the protective and healing power of beef tallow. In that interim period, I used coconut cooking oil. It wasn't the best option, as it was not pure coconut oil, but it was all the shift I could afford at the time. For light frying, like eggs, I used butter. For the few times I could afford to buy bacon, I saved all the drippings that I scraped off the pan. Today and for the past four years we've been using beef tallow in all our frying and sautéing.

5. Consider shifting to **ketogenic diet (J.1)**. Before you do, study as much as you can about it. I gave a lot of links on the subject in Chapter 11.

For my own family, most specially our youngest son, Jetross, ketogenic diet has done great improvements on his wellbeing. Jetross lost 22 pounds after 30 days of strict keto diet. And another 15 pounds after 10 months of mild ketosis. Emotionally and mentally, he is so much more stable and productive. He's not yet at his best, but he's surely not where he used to be.

If you are still stuck at guide number 4, thinking and feeling hopeless with the prospect of ditching your sugar addiction, then ketogenic diet is that addiction's Heel of Achilles. **Keto foods will help you forget about your romance with sugar, in just a matter of days**. As you will learn from the links I gave in Chapter 11, this is credited to the lasting and nourishing effects of natural animal fats - much unlike the fleeting, short-lived satisfaction processed sugar affords. It sustains not just your gut but also your brain.

When I started my husband and our two sons on ketogenic meals, it was only a matter of days when we noticed we were cooking and preparing meals less and less frequently. On our 20th or so days on keto, I served breakfast during lunch and seldom served dinner at all. They just stopped asking for more food! We were on "Intermittent Fasting" without even exerting an effort!

When we didn't feel like having full meals we would just snack on varied nuts like almonds, cashew and macadamia. What was amazing was we were much more energetic on keto than we ever were on carbohydrates. When we were exercising, we sweat a lot but were not breathless.

But the most astonishing benefit we derived as a family from this high fat diet was psychological and emotional. **There were suddenly much less arguments and more compassion and willingness to understand the other person. The peace that we had was not**

easily disturbed the way it used to be by simple offenses like careless words or gestures.

I strongly encourage you to try keto. Yet don't just take my word for it. To inspire you to do more of your own study, I've written hereunder a few of the most significant benefits you can get from a ketogenic diet as related to depression and anxiety disorder.

By the way you don't have to feel threatened by the idea that it's a "lifetime marriage or nothing". You can do keto for as short as a month or a year or longer, depending on your goals. Whichever length of time you choose, you are bound to reap its benefits. And let the benefits help you decide as to whether you will continue, stop for a while, or make it your lifestyle.

Benefits of Ketogenic Diet in relation to depression and anxiety disorders:

a. When on ketogenic diet, the body produces more Gamma-Aminobutyric acid (GABA). When the brain's GABA levels are enough, it has more stability, calm, focus, and the ability to concentrate is higher. **Thus, it's easier to start and finish a task in a shorter period. This is very important because anxiety and depression can easily make a person give up in the middle of a task.**

b. On a ketogenic diet, the brain uses Ketones as its primary source of fuel. Ketones are the brain's preferred source of fuel (not glucose, nor sugar. nor carbohydrates) and that has been so for most of man's time on Earth. **Feeding the brain its preferred fuel translates to long-lasting mental and physical energy that is not easily susceptible to breakdown or fatigue.** While on ketosis, I can achieve varied tasks, physical and mental, one after the other, and still not feel short on energy.

c. On Ketones, our cells are much more satiated and energized on levels that don't fluctuate. **The consistency and dependability of this**

energy source is manifested into much less mood swings and irritability. The whole family can take advantage of this benefit. My husband, on a high-carb diet must have at least three major meals in a day. Otherwise, he gets easily short-tempered. But on high-fat ketogenic diet, he can go on two meals a day, sometimes one, without any irritability.

It is crucial to note that despite the existence of a huge amount of anecdotal evidences boosting the validity of ketogenic diet's effectivity in managing depression, there are also minimal occurrences of depressed people who didn't recover from depression at all. I have also read about some who were depressed, recovered after being on keto and then relapsed back to depression even while still on keto. It is my hope that scientific studies be done on this issue to find the underlying physiological factors that prevent some depressed patients from experiencing the same healing and recovery experienced by most.

However, I would like to offer my humble speculation that the key element is "balance". Everything an individual need to be at his optimum level should be available in his body.

For example, if someone with depression and high blood pressure switches to keto, but does not get sufficient sun exposure, is low on potassium, doesn't exercise and refuses to cut down on coffee, then his HBP will most likely stay up.

This is the same with the rest of the nutrients needed by the body. If the body is depleted in any of these nutrients, it will initially try to compensate. When it reaches the point when compensation isn't enough to keep the scale balanced, manifestations of this lack will appear. **This is the body's defense mechanism to keep you from entering the inflammation stage.** This is what happened to me when I felt those persistent food cravings even after having crawled out of my depression pit two years before. The nutrients I got from the bottles of supplements my sister gave me soon got depleted as I rejoined the world and started performing my duties as mother, wife and business owner. It was as if I was like being constantly followed by the shadow of depression. There was a perpetual sense of mild foreboding.

It was only after I responded to these food cravings when the "shadow" stopped following me and I no longer felt threatened even when under a significant amount of stress.

CHAPTER 7: REALIZE THAT STRESSES ARE HERE TO STAY

Mild to severe stresses are part of today's realities. We can try to avoid or minimize them, but we would be **better off** if we are prepared - physically, mentally, emotionally and spiritually - when we face them.

Some say that our generation faces the worst levels of stresses that mankind has ever had to deal with. In my opinion, a more accurate reflection would be: **Today's human, with his severely compromised state of wellbeing, has never been more vulnerable to the effects of stresses**.

We feel helpless in facing these stresses, not because they are too strong for us but because we have become too weak for them. We have become exposed and defenseless. **With this system of defenses down, stresses become insurmountable and we are overwhelmed by depression. But when our defenses are in place with their integrity intact, depression need not be the "default avenue" for us.**

PAY CONSTANT ATTENTION TO YOUR BODY'S SOUND BITES

When I craved for sun exposure, raw milk, beef fats, butter, chicken feet, chicken skin, avocados, coconut meat and coconut water, "Balut", my favorite greens and fruits, and so forth, my brain and body were screaming:

"We're in desperate need of the right kind of fuel! We need fats, short-chain fatty acids from resistant carbs, and oh yes, some protein. We need what we are mostly made of! We are not made of simple carbohydrates! We are dying because you've been feeding us the wrong stuff, and the worst kind! Come on! We need the stuff that make us thrive! And until you feed us properly, we are going to wreak havoc! You've given us no choice! Either we do that, or you perish with us!".

The inflammation stage that my body went through was its way of "wreaking havoc". It was its amplifier that sounded the alarms round-the-clock. **It forced me to stop and listen.** My body wanted to heal and repair itself. Soon the cravings became so prominent they couldn't be ignored.

Through all the cravings I experienced, my body was making sure that it healed and repaired itself with the right building materials that will make it last longer and withstand the same or more intense sources of stress.

When this 'bill of materials' was satisfied, and the healing crew could finally do their job with the much needed and now available resources, my cravings gradually subsided.

For far too long, we have entrusted our wellbeing in the hands of our doctors, the government and the capitalists led by the big pharma - the medicine manufacturers. We have believed everything they propagated hook, line, and sinker. We have been cajoled into a corner, persuaded that there's no need for us to use our judicious mind, and that it is for our own benefit that we just accepted their recommendations, wholly and uncritically, because, as they claim, they have only our best interests in mind.

PRACTICAL GUIDE:

Study. Educate yourself.

There is no person more responsible in restoring your body's defenses than yourself. You are the top man for the job. **The very first step in restoring your defenses is educating yourself.** Living in this age of internet, all you need to know with regards to how best to restore your health defense system (primarily your digestive health), is literally at your fingertips.

Stresses will never stop coming. Rebuild your body's defenses, so that when stresses come, you have a fighting chance of withstanding them. **Give in to your body's truest cravings.** It is showing you the appropriate building materials your defenses need.

CHAPTER 8: THE BILL OF MATERIALS: MY HEALING CREW

Notes:

1. You will find all the diagrams in Chapter 12.
2. The alphanumericals written at the right side of the nutrients represent its bullet heading in Chapter 11.

Diagram 1 – Raw Milk

I felt the very first cravings for raw milk when I was about 8 years old. My body was already sending signals of the coming onslaught of skin allergies and eventually, asthma. These two presented themselves 30 years later from when the cravings started

First, I had a very bad case of mouth sores which was extremely painful. There were sores under my upper lip, lower lip, under the tongue, and in between my molars and cheeks. A couple of months later, very itchy eczema ridges on my lower legs started appearing. Then a year later I developed severe allergic rhinitis. A few weeks later, the allergic rhinitis gave birth to full blown asthma. That was in 2012.

I was prescribed with drugs including 2 kinds of inhalers. I had 3 kinds of wheezing lung sounds which my pulmonologist regarded as the worst he had heard from patients my age. After taking the meds and finishing several inhalers, I was not any better. I craved raw milk again and fortunately by this period we could afford to set a budget for several liters on a regular basis. I consumed raw milk and ate beef fats and salmon and stopped all medications for asthma. I avoided the worst allergens like yellow food colorings (which my pulmonologist never mentioned), other food additives, and pollens. My improvement was very gradual with lots of relapses each time I ingested a strong allergen.

Had I given in to these raw milk cravings when I first felt them at age 8, I would not have succumbed to these skin allergies and respiratory conditions. I was thankful though that these allergies and asthma manifested themselves after I recovered from depression as it would have made everything much worse physically.

How about raw milk and depression? Since the human body's cells is 90% bacteria and raw milk is loaded with healing and powerful probiotics, healthy fats, vitamins and minerals, could I have recovered from depression much quickly had I given in to my raw milk cravings early enough? Or even better, could it have prevented me from "entering" depression had it been given a chance to heal my inflamed gut and brain as early as age 8?

Could it have helped my gut and brain communicate in a better way, by:
1. providing the needed vitamins and minerals and making them bio-available;
2. by being a good source of tryptophan, which helps our brain produce feel-good chemicals;
3. by providing fat-soluble vitamins (A, D and K2) that naturally help balance the hormones;

4. by providing both omega 3 fatty acids and short-chain fatty acids that help feed the gut, manage stress and inflammation and control metabolism;
5. by providing loads of electrolytes (calcium, magnesium, potassium) which control and regulate, among others, high blood pressure?

Could it? JUST ASKING.

Diagram 2 - SALMON
Diagram 3 - Beef Fats, "Balut", Chicken Skin, Pork Skin/Fat
Around the same time that I started to give in to intense cravings for salmon and juicy beef meat and fats, my husband started to complain of stomach pains from his ulcers. Still financially constrained to set a budget for doctor consultations and medications, I opted to research about how he can be relieved and heal from ulcers. Amazingly, I discovered that natural fats and collagen are the best natural sources for repair materials that heal a damaged gut lining.

After finding a local source of beef fats (suet) by the bulk, I bought 8 kilos. Back at home, I cut them up in small pieces and started to fry to render the fats. The rendered fat is called "tallow" and this will be our cooking oil since then. Also, the resulting cracklings after rendering the fats tasted so good and we snacked on them while they were warm. Eating these beef fat cracklings can make my salivary glands go crazy.

One time, while I was frying the fats, a former housekeeper came by for a visit and she saw me with my cut-up kilos of beef suet on the kitchen counter. Without me having to explain what I was doing, Manang Delia said, *"You know Mam, in our province, beef fats are what our elders used to cure those with stomach ulcers and those who lose their minds."* I was gobsmacked! I stared at her a long while. I couldn't believe what I just heard. Wasn't I suffering from a mental condition? Wasn't Jet suffering from ulcers? And wasn't those the reasons why I was rendering the suet for tallow and cracklings for our consumption? I interviewed her for the next hour and everything I learned from her completely sealed the cracks of doubts around whether how I was dealing with our family's health was right at all.

How could our ancestors, without books or internet or television or any of the modern tools we use for learning, had known what was good for them and their ailments? They just knew. They were so in tuned with their symbiotic relationship with nature, and their intuition had remained unburdened and undefiled by the modern concept of health and medicines. This strong and natural intuition was not weakened by the convenient availability of medical doctors, that we, in contrast to these traditional and provincial inhabitants, have resorted to, both for small and big aches and pains in our body. **This God-given, nature-endowed sensitivity is what we need to re-awaken in us.** In my case, I first needed to be stripped of all provisions which left me unable to gravitate towards medical doctors and medicines. Having torn down all those barriers between "me" and my health, or should I say "ill-health", I was finally able to communicate with my body and finally able to "listen" to what it was it had been telling me that it needed to heal.

Another thing was my intense cravings for juicy and fatty beef meat. Oh, that one truly exasperated me! I'd stay awake at night, profusely salivating over non-stop thoughts of thick, plump juicy cheeseburgers with multiple layers of beef patties. I felt so torn and helpless because the budget was very tight that I could hardly manage to send my sons to school with enough food in their lunch boxes. I can't remember how I eventually got over these cravings, but it always took so much willpower for me not to run off and burn our full day's food budget for a burger at the nearest burger joint.

As a young girl, I have always had anemia. And recently, after bouts of nausea, my lab revealed that my ferritin storage is almost empty. Ferritin is the protein in our organ's cells, like liver, that stores iron. There are now emerging studies, as well as anecdotal evidences that link depression to low levels of ferritin. One fast way to bump up your body's low levels of ferritin is, guess what, by eating red meat!

Was that intense craving for red meat my body's way of avoiding depression?

These days, although it is very seldom that I experience strong cravings for animal fats, I am conscious of my appreciation and preference for them when faced with a varied assortment of dishes, like at a buffet restaurant. Even if I had planned to immediately feast on some "carbs" like pizza, or pasta or desserts, I always end up filling up my very first buffet plate with grilled salmon jaw, steak slices with thick layers of fat, chicken feet and stewed pig's feet (*Pata Tim*). That plate is almost always followed by a fruit plate filled with slices of watermelon (*Pakwan*) which serve as my thirst-quenching water during the entire meal and a few slices of ripe mango. If I ever stood up for a piece of dessert it was usually merely out of curiosity after seeing so many neighbors indulging on them. I am being completely honest with you when I say that this behavior is purely out of intuition, **a deep but subconscious awareness in me that it will provide me both gratification and satiety, and second only to that is the now "experiential knowledge" that eating such food can only be good for me.** There is no "struggle" in me or the need to "stay disciplined" and choose these types of food. I gravitate toward them and the **peace and satisfaction that come after serve to validate the wisdom of my food nutrition choices.**

ON "BALUT"
"Baluuuuuuuut! Baluuuuuuuut!"

At the street where I grew up in Manila, that was a nightly staple call made by the area's "*magbabalut*", heard around 7pm to 10pm, as he walked up and down our street. These days, we'd have to go out to the village gate where the magbabalut is stationed, from as early 5pm to until his balut supply lasted. The villagers either bring home their hot balut fare to enjoy with the rest of the family or eat them right there by the vendor's warm basket of balut from where they may get one of its dangling vinegar bottles.

Balut is a boiled 16-to-21-day-old fertilized duck egg (or chicken egg). To eat, the flatter end of the egg is cracked and peeled; a grain of salt or chili is sprinkled along with a few drops of vinegar and then the mild, yet delicious soup is sipped through the crack; then the shell is peeled further down, and the rest of the egg is eaten.

Unlike the strong cravings I felt for beef meat/fats which started right in the middle of my depression, the ones I felt for balut were mild, though still persistent, and started around the same time as my cravings for squash seeds, more than a year before my depression started.

I craved for balut consistently a few days a week. The funny thing about it was that after I had consumed 2 pieces of balut, I felt like I didn't want to eat it for a long time after that. And yet the craving was back a night or two later.

What was it with balut that my body needed? Balut is loaded with vitamins and minerals but it's being **rich in cholesterol** that my body recognized and craved for.

Here's a snippet from the **Cholesterol: Friend Or Foe A.2.35)?**, written by Natasha Campbell-McBride for the Weston A. Price Foundation website:

"Cholesterol is an integral and very important part of our cell membranes, the membranes that enclose each of our cells, and also of the membranes surrounding all the organelles inside the cell.... This ability of cholesterol and saturated fats to firm up and reinforce the tissues in the body is used by our blood vessels, particularly those that have to withstand the high pressure and turbulence of the blood flow. These are usually large or medium arteries in places where they divide or bend. The flow of blood pounding through these arteries forces them to incorporate a layer of cholesterol and saturated fat in the membranes, which makes it stronger, tougher and more rigid. These layers of cholesterol and fat are called fatty streaks. They are completely normal and form in all of us, starting from birth and sometimes even before we are born. Various indigenous populations around the world, who never suffer from heart disease, have plenty of fatty streaks in their blood vessels in old and young, including children. Fatty streaks are not indicative of the disease called atherosclerosis."

Since cholesterol is an integral part of our blood vessels that enables them to withstand the strong current of blood passing continually through them, could it be that the constant pounding I heard in my chest 24/7 was depleting my cholesterol supply? Which then caused me to crave for foods loaded with cholesterol such as Balut and animal fats?

Also, since I started craving for Balut as early as more than a year before my depression started, was my brain and gut preparing me for the onslaught that was to come?

However, our body can produce cholesterol whenever it needs to. It can convert protein and carbohydrates into cholesterol. The liver, our body's cholesterol "factory" does this job on a full-time basis because cholesterol performs a multi-faceted function in our body, 24/7.

This means that I should have been able to produce cholesterol and top-up any cholesterol deficiency I might have had, right? **The answer is yes, provided that the liver has the materials needed to do the conversion job**. The liver is particularly busy with cholesterol production whenever the body shifts the gear from inflammation to healing, most particularly that stage of healing when an injured tissue recreates.

Could my intense and seemingly irrational cravings for fatty meats and my long-term craving for cholesterol-laden Balut, being driven by my body's need to heal and recreate damaged cells? Could my liver be helping send signals to my brain **to compel me** to consume either enough dietary cholesterol or the raw materials for it, to make sure that it wasn't disturbed from making enough cholesterol that my body was demanding for its healing?

Vitamin D is a vital vitamin in healing depression. When the skin is exposed to the sunlight, it is the cholesterol underneath it that is primarily used to manufacture Vitamin D. When I felt rejuvenated emotionally, mentally and physically, as soon as I was exposed to the sun, it showed how deficient I was with vitamin D. Could the cravings for cholesterol-rich foods my body's way of prepping itself to make sure it could make Vitamin D as soon as it was prompted?

Diagram 4 – Avocado

Diagram 5 - Coconut Oil/Meat/Water

Diagram 6 - Leafy Greens "Kangkong, Talbos Ng Kamote, Petchay" (Water Spinach, Cabbage, Sweet Potato Tops)

Diagram 7 - Beef Tendons, Chicken Feet, "Buto ng Pakwan at Kalabasa" (Watermelon and Squash Seeds)

When I craved and indulged in bowls and bowls of **squash and watermelon seeds P.5**, **chicken feet H.5**, and apples, it was about the same time as when I first started to experience what uncontrolled anxiety felt like.

It was the year 2005-2006 and I was heavily into badminton. I would do very well during practices but when I played during competitions, my knees felt weak and my wrists were limp, and I could hardly keep a tight grip around the racket from the sweat my palms were excreting. As a result, I avoided smashing the shuttlecock and relied on drop shots instead. I couldn't understand it. I loved and enjoyed the game and I longed to be fearless during the competitions just as I felt during practices.

I was not unfamiliar with anxiety. I felt a lot of anxiety when I was younger, back in the university, during exams and presentations, but that kind of anxiety always carried me through to positive results. This time, it was a kind of anxiety that left me breathless, sweaty, weak, overwhelmed and fearing something I loved to do.

With what I know now about the relationship between gut health/dysbiosis and anxiety and fear, I wonder if all those cravings I felt for squash seeds, and apples and chicken feet were my body's way of trying to fend off a coming inflammation? Or was I already inflamed and trying to heal and my cravings for those foods' nutrients were my body's way of saying:

"Hey Rose! We need some raw mats down here! You know, for repair work on your gut lining? And your gut diversity, well, it's NOT diverse anymore. So, it would really help if you could ingest more of those nutrients. More! More!"

PRACTICAL GUIDE:

If you still feel at a loss and can't seem to distinguish between false cravings and true ones, then look at the foods that I craved for. The set of nutrients my body derived from these foods are universal raw materials that can help repair and restore any person's gut diversity and overall digestive health, which you now know, directly affect the immune system and the brain, thus our mental health.

As you start to provide your body these much-needed raw materials, your inflamed organs, including your brain, will latch on to these raw materials and immediately commence the healing and regeneration process. You will feel the positive lift in your mood and emotions as these nutrients start to do their job both in your gut and brain. When that 2-way line of communication between your gut and brain is re-established, you will be able to determine, through actual experiences and cravings, how these nutrients benefit your body.

Hold on to this accumulating experiential knowledge and continually respond to your nutrient cravings. Healing from depression is an ongoing process that goes way beyond your exit from the pit.

CHAPTER 9: SHOULD I STILL ASK: WHY ME?

The question "How did I heal from depression?" has been answered.

There is another that demands equal attention:
"Why did I suffer from depression?", or "Why **me**?"

Now we know that that question cannot be answered by:
"Because I had too much stress"; nor
"I made a lot of mistakes";

Both reasons are **not the causes** of my depression.
They were just **"triggers"**.

I know of other people who have faced much greater stresses in life and made much worse mistakes but never ever exhibited any signs of depression. Their wall didn't even crack.

I, however, entered the arena of depression with a very weak wall of defense – one that had a lot of holes in it. We can even take that phrase literally - I had an inflamed and leaky gut that weakened my immune system. When stresses came, the nutritional dregs I was running on, very quickly depleted. I dried up. The engine stopped. I was immobilized by the frightening characteristics of depression.

My depression stayed even when the stresses left; and even after I stopped making bad decisions. Healing started when I finally gave in to my body's true cravings. When I provided the raw materials needed to heal, it sealed the leaks in my gut and restarted my immune system.

The science behind my recovery cannot be denied. Through studies, such as: ***The Role of Nutrients in Protecting Mitochondrial Function and Neurotransmitter Signaling: Implications for the Treatment of Depression, PTSD, and Suicidal Behaviors* A.1.1)**, we understand why and how nutritional therapy is the most effective solution for depression and suicidal tendencies.

But I want to know if this road to depression truly started with being nutritionally deficient and having a leaky gut. Was that really the very start of that road for me, and for many others suffering from depression?

Or is that road hiding an earlier stretch?

Why bother ask these questions??? I healed from depression. I know why and how I healed. Isn't that what counts the most? All anyone needs to do is to make sure that they address their nutritional deficiencies and heal their leaky gut, and soon they will emerge from their depression pit.

NO. I am not prepared to settle with that.

I want to find out what brought the possibility of depression for me.

What exactly **qualified** me to be depressed.

Why **me**?

If we can answer these questions, then we can avoid so many heartaches and tragedies. We can save lives and give them chance to fulfill their potentials.

Nutritional therapy **doesn't have to be a therapy**.

It will simply be **a way of life.**

At the initial stages of my quest to answer those questions, much of what I learned was from **"Stress & The Gut-Brain Axis: Regulation By The Microbiome"A.1.2)** . The following is a portion of the paper's abstract:

"The importance of the gut-brain axis in regulating stress-related responses has long been appreciated. More recently, the microbiota has emerged as a key player in the control of this axis, especially during conditions of stress provoked by real or perceived homeostatic challenge. Diet is one of the most important modifying factors of the microbiota-gut-brain axis. The routes of communication between the microbiota and brain are slowly being unraveled, and include the vagus nerve, gut hormone signaling, the immune system, tryptophan metabolism, and microbial metabolites such as short chain fatty acids. The importance of the early life gut microbiota in shaping later health outcomes also is emerging. <u>Results from preclinical studies indicate that alterations of the early microbial composition by way of antibiotic exposure, lack of breastfeeding, birth by Caesarean section, infection, stress exposure, and other environmental influences - coupled with the influence of host genetics - can result in long-term modulation of stress-related physiology and behaviour.</u>"

As soon as I read the last part, I felt overwhelmed. Because this study, along with many others like it, proved that, indeed, **my road to depression started much earlier than my being nutritionally deficient.**

Let me explain by walking you through a journey that started on the day I was born, or possibly even during gestation.

CHAPTER 10: THE LONG, EARLY AND SURE ROAD TO MY DEPRESSION

Please do take time to explore all of the referenced words and phrases. The three digits after each referenced phrase/word represent the bullet headings of that topic/title which are all listed in Chapter 11.

I pray that you finish the chapter and absorb as much as you can from it. It will help you and many others you know who are also living with these conditions.

THE EARLY ROAD TO MY DEPRESSION

I was the youngest of 8 children. As early as the 4th child, Mama had wanted to separate from Papa due to his never-ending philandering. My godmother who lived next door to us was witness to most of their altercations and the **emotional turmoil Mama enduredA.2.1)**.

By the time Mama conceived with me, tension at home was at its peak - Mama was constantly angry whenever Papa came home, either drunk or penniless from overnight gambling, or both. One of the earliest memories I had of them being both at home was a flat iron flying past over my head towards Papa who was bolting for the door. Our door was a thick, wooden

61

antique kind and the tip of the flat iron made a deep dent into the left frame just as Papa safely disappeared through the gap.

For the first 7 children Mama gave birth normally. When it was my turn, the doctor informed my parents that I was too big for normal delivery. I came out **through caesarianA.2.3) operationA.2.2)**. My birthweight was **9.8 poundsA.2.4)**, the average weight of a 3-month old baby. Mama indulged on **fruit salad iced-candiesA.2.5)** during most of her gestation period, and she was pre-diabetic by the time she delivered me (and insulin dependent in her late 50s). Mama was 40 years old when she gave birth to me.

By the time I came out, life in the family and business was much better than first experienced by my siblings. And much busier. Papa had a thriving business in which Mama was beginning to be an essential hand. Being active in the business, having 7 prior children to care for, then having to heal from the caesarian delivery, Mama decided to hire a nurse and a nanny to care for me. The nurse cared for me for just a few weeks as she trained the nanny who took care of me until I was in 2nd grade.

I didn't benefit from the lasting immunological advantage of **being born vaginallyA.2.6)** as well as from being nursed with my **mother's milkA.2.7)**. I grew up on **formulaA.2.8)** which I loved even as a grade schooler. I can still remember laying my head on my nanny's lap in my school's cafeteria sucking my milk bottle during recess and lunch. I was 8 years old. I was very happy to have my milk bottle to care for the stares both from students and teachers.

At home, my favorite meal was rice paired with **TocinoA.2.9)**, a sweetened, reddish, fried cuts of pork. I remember insisting that my nanny fry my rice in the oil she used to fry the Tocino. I refused to eat the meal if my rice wasn't "greasy and red" enough. During this time, late '70s, **vegetable oilA.2.10)** was the "in" oil.

I was almost 9 when my nanny left. We left the house I grew up in and I came to live with Mama at our shop. We had our living quarters at the second floor. The building was on a busy and polluted commercial street. Soon after we relocated, I became constantly **nauseous and dizzyA.2.11)**. Tests soon showed I had **anemiaA.2.12)**. I took an iron-rich multi-vitamin for many years. It was supposed to aid my nausea. But I felt much better after having drunk a half-liter of **raw milkA.2.13)** which would occasionally arrive from our province.

Raw milk was the only thing that trumped how much I regarded my formula milk bottle. I cannot recall if I had let anybody in the family know how I felt about raw milk. All I know was that it soon stopped coming.

I was also made to eat **liverA.2.14)** cooked in different ways. Simply-fried pork or chicken liver was the best, I thought. I remember the first time I was to eat liver, Mama tried to promote its many benefits to me and how good it supposedly tasted. But the obvious publicity just made me anticipate the opposite. Before this time, liver was not part of my daily diet nor that of my siblings'. But I was prepared to try it to ease my constant nausea. When I took my first bite of a fried pork liver, I was surprised by how much I liked it. It was warm, juicy and most of all, tasty.

I was 12 when Mama started to bring me to **DivisoriaA.2.15)**. It's a huge complex of buildings in the heart of Manila where she bought all the materials for our tailoring business. The building where the fabrics were displayed and marketed was a very smelly maze of stalls, through which Mama dragged me as she conversed with her suppliers, waited for her orders to be packed and made the payments. This process took from 2 to 3 hours, 2 to 3x a week.

There was not a walk through those chemical-smelling networks of **textile stallsA.2.16)** that didn't make me nauseous, my eyes watery from irritation, my throat to close up and my **head to throb with pain for hoursA.2.17).** The time came when I dreaded going inside that building.

One day, just as Mama and I were about to enter the complex, I got a whiff of the chemical smell and promptly felt nauseous. I pulled Mama's arm back and begged her to just let me stay outside and promised to wait for her. She entrusted me to one of the Chinese suppliers she knew who had an outside stall and I sat there until Mama came out 2 hours later.

This period, from when I started to live with Mama at our shop, to when I was about 14-15 years old, was when I was sick most often. Each time I had fever or persistent cough, **antibioticsA.2.18)** were always part of my pediatrician's protocol for me. I remember hearing his constant reminder, to whomever brought me to his clinic, to "make sure I finish the entire 7-day antibiotics course". I didn't know then why that was important, but I do remember stopping taking the **medicinesA.2.19)** after 2 or 3 days since I had felt better.

There was no one to monitor if I had finished each course. Mama was busy with the business and all except one of my siblings had either gotten married and left home, or away in a school dormitory. Equally significant is the fact that I never once heard from my pediatrician, nor anyone else, that I was supposed to replenish my gut's health with **probiotics and supportive dietA.2.20)** after a course of antibiotics. Although probiotics were being explored as early as 1920s, it was only in 1980s when the "idea" started to gain traction. The very first time I heard about it was from my own son's pediatrician (1990s). She gave me a list of specific foods that I was supposed to give my son right after finishing his course of antibiotics.

Around thirteen years old, I started having facial acne. It was not so bad, but I was so bothered by the itchiness which made it hard to resist the urge to touch or scratch my face. I was brought to a dermatologist who made me take **contraceptive pillsA.2.21)** to "balance my hormones" which was to help heal my acne.

64

By the time I was fifteen, more **odorsA.2.22)** triggered my nausea: exhaust fumes from **motor vehiclesA.2.23)**, petrol fumes from gasoline stations, newly-painted rooms and insecticides. I also didn't like the smell of the oil they put in the sewing machines of our sewers, especially when the sewing machines are at work and heating up the oils. At our new place, our bedrooms were adjacent to the sewing rooms. To get to the ground floor we always passed through the sewing room and so there was no escaping that **sewing oil smellA.2.24)**.

Also, there were lots of fabric rolls at the ground floor, where the retail area of our shop was located, which emitted that chemical fabric odor. When I was old enough, I was required to man the shop at least 3x a week. This is about the time I started to have persistent headaches. I remember preferring to sit at the fruit stand mama had right in front of the shop. I am relieved whenever I smell the fresh fruits

When I was 16, I developed a knack for charcoal painting. But some months into the hobby, I felt nauseous from the smell of the **fixative spray A.2.26)** I used to set the painting. So, I stopped the hobby.

On the other hand, I loved the smell of freshly-cut grass, trees, and the fresh smell of the ground after a heavy rain. Growing up in that commercial street, I enjoyed my forbidden trips to the hospital compound right across the street. The compound had lots of trees and among them were my favorite **AratilesA.2.28)** fruit trees. Being very skinny from 10 to 16 years old, I could climb up these trees and balance my limbs all the way to the outreaching branches to pick the tiny sweet and tart fruits. Mama forbade me from climbing these trees, but I enjoyed climbing the trees as much as eating the fruits. I never feared the promised spanking from Mama, which I always received after arriving with my basket of aratiles. Strangely, after my spanking, Mama allowed me to keep my aratiles stash in the refrigerator to cool. They tasted so much sweeter when eaten cold and I felt simply wonderful while and after eating them.

I also loved the **smell of apples and mangoesA.2.29)** and would press my nose on their skin to smell them before cutting to eat. I remember eating a full plate of sliced ripe, cold mangoes for my lunch and dinner and nothing else.

By age 16 I had at least 3 **root canalsA.2.30)** and 6 **amalgam fillingsA.2.31)**. I dreaded all those dental visits and I suffered from headaches after each one.

I was seventeen when **hair straighteningA.2.32)** salons became popular. Suddenly every natural-haired girl I knew wanted to have her hair straightened. I soon joined the bandwagon. I braved through the sickening salon odor for 2 to 3 hours at least once a year. My friends who had thicker hair made more frequent salon visits. While all of them remained jolly and talkative after the tiring long salon hours, I, on the other hand, was non-communicative and preferred to go straight home. I had headaches that lasted for days. Most of my friends followed the salon's instructions not to wash hair for 24 hours. I washed mine within 8 hours as I couldn't stand the itch on my scalp and the persistent chemical odor emanating from my scalp and hair.

Around late 1980s, buying and selling of imported second-hand clothes became popular. Mama decided to venture into this trending business. She brought me along with her to the depots where they kept those jumbo boxes of used clothing. We could rummage through the boxes before we decide which ones to buy. Once back at the shop, we sorted out the items and arranged them on hangers. Soon enough, I started feeling heady from the chemical scent which oozed out from the used-clothing. The initial excitement that I used to feel from the prospect of finding treasure items, such as branded blouses and denims, quickly became irrelevant. I dreaded the nauseating odor that gave me headaches for days. I didn't know then that these used clothes were heavily sprayed with **formaldehydeA.2.33)** to prevent mildew.

As I reached my late teen years, I became increasingly reclusive, preferring to read books - holed up in my room - if I wasn't in school. Going out in the polluted streets of Manila always made me feel lousy, emotionally and physically.

For my 18th birthday, Mama asked me to choose between having a big debutant party, which was customary in the Philippines, or buying my own car. I said I didn't care for either and asked instead for a weekend getaway in Boracay. Boracay is now our country's top tourist island destination in Western Visayas but was relatively unknown in the 1980s. More than the sights of that wondrous virgin island, I just wanted to soak myself in the clean smell of trees and the salty, breezy air.

Those five days were heaven to me. A storm had just passed a couple of days before we arrived, and the coastline was littered with coconut leaves, broken branches and split coconut pods as far as the eye could see. It was the untidiest yet prettiest mess I could ever behold. My eyes feasted on the restful beige, coffee and green colors of the beach and trees as they kissed each other. Everything smelled the way they should in my world, clean and light and nothing repulsive. I couldn't take in enough of the competing scents of the briny air and decaying twigs, dangling and waiting to be snapped free from their storm-tossed tree branches. In that nature's purest state, I spent hours without worry of nausea or headache. I dreaded for the trip's end to come and the day I was to inhale Manila's pollution once again.

I was 19 years old when I met Jet, my husband. It was my first time to fall in love and it seemed to have opened a pandora's box of other emotions I couldn't control. Soon after we got engaged, I was constantly enveloped in fits of jealousy. In each one, my mind rapidly filled up with irrational thoughts that often went out of control and inevitably turned a peaceful day into a hateful chaos.

Many even led to physical fights. After I have exhausted my energy in a fit of **rageA.2.34)**, I would wonder where the emotions had gone and how come I no longer felt them? Where were the worries that jumpstarted my rage, the jealousy? After every "episode", I felt ashamed for having blown out of proportion something that didn't matter at all. I felt I was living with another totally different and monstrous person inside me, whose aggression there was no telling when to rear its head up again. Up until this point, I had thought that there were things wrong only with my body, my physical being. Suddenly, being nauseous and withdrawn and having headaches were bumped down the list of my "subnormalities". And that list just took on a new name: "abnormalities".

Getting married and raising our sons kept my mind occupied and gave me and Jet some form of respite from my manic behavior. Though each lull became longer as years passed, Jet knew better than to let his guard down.

One time, we were out in a mall just walking past boutique windows, when I saw a very attractive lady around same age as me. I was stealing long glances at her, enjoying her appearance and how she moved. Then I shook Jet's arm and motioned him to look at the lady and excitedly whispered "She's so pretty sweetheart! Look at her." As soon he saw her, he immediately jerked his head away to the other direction. For a few seconds, I didn't understand; then it dawned on me. Oh, poor Jet! He must have thought I was playing a joke on him, or worse, laying down a trap! My crazy, vicious behavior had turned my cool, fun-loving husband into an anxious, overly-cautious paranoid. At that point, I stared hard at the real "me", who had just resurfaced, after years of being shoved down by my irrational, manic, jealous "other" persona. It was almost like hearing someone whisper "This is who you really are, Rose. You appreciate beauty, both in nature and in people. Do not forget that."

I wish I had the sense and presence of mind to analyze what had put the brakes on my mental and emotional avalanche. For example, were there changes in my diet and nutrition? I wasn't that perceptive yet. But I guess, it helped that I saw those two persons at the same time: the real me and the horrendous wannabe. I suddenly didn't want to have anything more to do with that wannabe.

Unfortunately, my resolve wasn't enough to help me keep my emotions and thoughts in constant check. Impulsiveness became a persistent, welcoming, and easier choice instead of staying sober, careful and analytical. This is the state mind and emotions I was in, back in 2007, when I made so many crucial decisions that eventually led to my descent into intense depression.

THE TRUE ROOT CAUSE OF MY DEPRESSION

I have read so many published studies, (including meta-analysis of various researches, books, internet articles, and professional online webinars), on what could have caused my depression and severe anxieties. I now have no doubt that I had set foot on the road to depression as early as my gestation (mainly affected by my mother's diet and emotional condition), or possibly even way before being conceived (how my parents' lifestyles impacted their sperm and egg).

However, it was:
1. being born via caesarian which gave me a gut microbiota deficient of the beneficial microbes I could have inherited through my mother's vaginal flora (depleted as it may have been due to many contributing factors, still, it would have been better than nothing);

2. not being nourished with my mother's milk, and worse, being hooked on formula milk for the first eight years of my life. This failed to nourish my gut with the probiotics that a mother's milk can give and encouraged the bad bacteria to flourish through the sugars from the formula.
3. living on basically nutrition-deprived food for most of my early years to early adulthood. This negated efforts my gut was making to create balance between the good and bad bacteria.

All these three, collectively, served as the primary key that opened the door to depression. These are what made the possibility of depression up and visible on the horizon.

But the "straw that broke the camel's back" is subjecting my already weak gut microbiota under the repeated and indiscriminate assaults of the following:

1. toxic, chemical and environmental pollutants;
2. mercury-laden dental fillings;
3. antibiotics, from childhood to adulthood,

All these, in a team work, was what shoved me right through the wide and open door of depression. All these components, one after another, and in some period even wreaking their havoc in a symphony, had finally overwhelmed my body's homeostasis; suddenly I didn't have enough of what was needed to function in the most basic way. I was drained to the core.

Conversely, had I been "whole", healthy and in a balanced state of functioning homeostasis, with my gut microbiota producing the appropriate chemicals of communication with my brain, I would not have fallen into the pit of depression; I would not have made so many mistakes; I would have handled things much differently.

LOST OPPORTUNITIES

In between those two stages in my life: from when I was born with a sterile gut, therefore, vulnerable immune system, all the way to 2007, when I was shoved into the pit of depression, was a long period of nonstop opportunities. Opportunities to "correct" the tipping scale, to douse the fire, to ease the inflammation, to heal.

From the time that I started to feel:

1. constant nausea,
2. having headaches,
3. craving for apples, mangoes, trees and nature,
4. to preferring isolation and quiet surroundings,
5. to feeling satiated by raw milk and craving for more,
6. to being overcome with intense feelings of jealousy and rage,
7. to having insomnia, chest pains, and intense anxieties,
8. to feeling utter despair alternating with pure dread,
9. to having suicidal thoughts and just wanting to disappear and escape for good,

- to suddenly wanting to soak in the sun, and eat salmon, beef fats, and all those other nutritious foods - **these were all the opportunities, the signals, being sent by whatever remained in my dying gut microbes, into my brain, in their efforts to get help, to survive.**

Finally, they got my attention, though rather not-so-consciously at first. And then I started to heal.

Following are diagrams that I hope have organized all those factors that I have pointed out. They detail all the influences at each stage of my life leading to that stage when I entered depression.

(The diagrams can be viewed in the Diagrams and Gallery section of the book.)

Diagram 8: Pre-Gestational

Diagram 9 – Gestational

Diagram 10 – Birth and Early Feeding

Diagram 11 – Early Childhood to Adulthood

* * *

I was born with sterile and compromised gut microbiota, therefore, a compromised immune system that was further and repeatedly injured by my lifelong poor diet and exposure to various toxins.

December 30, 1970 was the day I was born. December 2007 was the time I first started to feel the very first signs of depression and intense anxieties. By January 2008, I was almost completely immobilized by these manifestations. In between these 2 periods is the long road my body traveled towards debilitating depression and severe anxieties.

Over the years, as I trekked on this long road to depression, it proved to be a road that had so many avenues branching out of it. **These avenues were the "opportunities" that were being presented to me along the way to give me a chance to get off the road to depression and onto the road to health.**

These "opportunities" presented themselves both in the form of ill-health manifestations (nausea, severe headaches, hypothyroidism, weight problems, skin problems, cancer, asthma, etc.) and intense cravings for nutrition that could have helped reverse these manifestations.

But when my feet stayed on the sure and wide road to depression, eventually, I touched down.

Enveloped in depression and intense anxieties, though immobilized, my body continued to fight. It refused to surrender. It didn't stop sending its SOS, on and on and on. In my dark and isolated cocoon of despair, these soundbites eventually reached whatever functioning part of my brain remained, and finally, I responded to those aggressive nutritional cravings.

You know the rest of the story.

PRACTICAL GUIDE:

Whether you're holding this book because you have reached the end of that long road and are now suffering from depression or whether you can tell that you are on your way, you need not wait.

Look on your left and on your right. Try to see those avenues that are now branching out to show you the way out of your own depression. However, instead of focusing on ill-health manifestations (eczema, headaches, anxieties), focus instead on your body's attempts to instruct you on how to recover.

For example, what nutritional cravings are you experiencing? Pay attention. Listen. Do you feel better and rejuvenated when you're out in nature and breathing fresh air? Listen. Do you feel worse after exposing yourself to something toxic (pollution, processed food)? Listen. Do you feel a strong desire for a certain nutritious food and can't seem to get enough of? Listen.

It took me 37 years trekking this long and sure road to depression; it's quite impractical of me to expect to "stay" healed from it after just a few months of nutritional rehabilitation.

Mull over these quotations by Hippocrates, the Father of Modern Medicine:

"Everyone has a doctor in him or her; we just have to help it in its work."

"The natural healing force within each one of us is the greatest force in getting well."

"Our food should be our medicine. Our medicine should be our food."

"Leave your drugs in the chemist's pot if you can heal the patient with food."

CHAPTER 11: RESOURCES, MATERIALS AND CITATIONS

NOTE: What you have read so far, from Introduction to Chapter 10, comprises just the "tip" of the iceberg of information included in this book. The rest of this vital set of knowledge is right under this intro. I implore you to browse the headings and see what interest you the most. To read on the topic online, type the full text of either the title or hyperlink into your internet browser and press enter..

There is no better way to spend any leisure time you have than by absorbing these truths in. It is the only way to push out the lies that have permeated our minds about mental health.

For example, do you know that a certain study showed that those who tried to commit suicide are very deficient in Vitamin D?

See? I also didn't know that until I came across that study.

What we've been repeatedly told as the main culprit was "too much stress" or "chemical imbalance" or "genes".

You can find the link to this under **"On Sunlight, Vitamin D and Depression" C.1.**

A. Chapter Materials

1. Chapter 9: Should I still ask: Why me?
    1) The Role of Nutrients in Protecting Mitochondrial Function and Neurotransmitter Signaling: Implications for the Treatment of Depression, PTSD, and Suicidal Behaviors https://www.ncbi.nlm.nih.gov/pmc/articles/PMC4417658/
    2) Stress & the gut-brain axis: Regulation by the microbiome https://www.sciencedirect.com/science/article/pii/S2352289516300509?via%3Dihub

2. Chapter 10: The Long, Early and Sure Road to My Depression
    1) Antenatal maternal stress and long-term effects on child neurodevelopment: how and why? https://www.ncbi.nlm.nih.gov/pubmed/17355398
    2) 15 Ways A C-Section Negatively Affects The Baby https://www.babygaga.com/15-ways-a-c-section-negatively-affects-the-baby/
    3) Cesarean versus Vaginal Delivery: Long term infant outcomes and the Hygiene Hypothesis https://www.ncbi.nlm.nih.gov/pmc/articles/PMC3110651/ Neu J, Rushing J. Cesarean versus Vaginal Delivery: Long term infant outcomes and the Hygiene Hypothesis. Clinics in perinatology. 2011;38(2):321-331. doi:10.1016/j.clp.2011.03.008.
    4) Long-term consequences for offspring of diabetes during pregnancy

https://academic.oup.com/bmb/article/60/1/173/322735 Frans A Van Assche, Kathleen Holemans, Leona Aerts; Long-term consequences for offspring of diabetes during pregnancy, *British Medical Bulletin*, Volume 60, Issue 1, 1 November 2001, Pages 173–182, https://doi.org/10.1093/bmb/60.1.173

5) High fat, high sugar diet during pregnancy 'programs' for health complications in mother and child https://www.cam.ac.uk/research/news/high-fat-high-sugar-diet-during-pregnancy-programs-for-health-complications-in-mother-and-child

6) Delivery mode shapes the acquisition and structure of the initial microbiota across multiple body habitats in newborns https://www.ncbi.nlm.nih.gov/pmc/articles/PMC2900693/ Dominguez-Bello MG, Costello EK, Contreras M, et al. Delivery mode shapes the acquisition and structure of the initial microbiota across multiple body habitats in newborns. *Proceedings of the National Academy of Sciences of the United States of America.* 2010;107(26):11971-11975. doi:10.1073/pnas.1002601107.

7) A Breastfeeding Saga https://www.westonaprice.org/health-topics/childrens-health/a-breastfeeding-saga/

8) The Scandal of Infant Formula: A Poor Replacement for Mother's Milk https://www.westonaprice.org/health-

topics/childrens-health/the-scandal-of-infant-formula/

9) Tocino https://en.wikipedia.org/wiki/Tocino

10)   The Great Con-ola
https://www.westonaprice.org/health-topics/know-your-fats/the-great-con-ola/

11)   Iron-Deficiency Anemia
https://www.nhlbi.nih.gov/health-topics/iron-deficiency-anemia

12)   Iron Deficiency Anemia
https://www.healthline.com/health/iron-deficiency-anemia

13)   THE MANY BENEFITS OF RAW MILK
https://www.realmilk.com/many-benefits-raw-milk/

14)   Liver: nature's most potent superfood
https://chriskresser.com/natures-most-potent-superfood/

15)   The Ultimate Guide To Divisoria
https://www.amommabroad.com/blog/2017/10/17/divisoria

16)   Toxicity concealed inside the Chemicals used in Textiles
https://www.textiletoday.com.bd/toxicity-concealed-inside-the-chemicals-used-in-textiles/

17)   Extreme Chemical Sensitivity Makes Sufferers Allergic to Life: Its sufferers were once dismissed as hypochondriacs, but there's growing biological evidence to explain toxicant-induced loss of tolerance (TILT)

http://discovermagazine.com/2013/nov/13-allergic-life

18) Restoring Gut Health After Antibiotic Use - Dr. Tom O'Bryan
https://www.youtube.com/watch?v=yxX8MlZN8Ws

19) Gut Health After Antibiotics Part 2 - Dr. Tom O'Bryan
https://www.youtube.com/watch?v=QL8rBn6L-Tg

20) LIVE How to Support Gut After Antibiotics, by Dr Josh Axe
https://www.youtube.com/watch?v=ePLznQsp52s

21) 7 Reasons To Go Off The Pill: The Truth About Birth Control Pill Side Effects: This inside look into hormonal birth control uncovers the scary truth about birth control pills and the serious side effects, like increased cancer risk, digestion disorders, and fertility issues.
https://rootandrevel.com/birth-control-pill-side-effects/

22) Multiple Chemical Sensitivity: Myth or Reality? https://www.questia.com/magazine/1G1-13996656/multiple-chemical-sensitivity-myth-or-reality

23) Toxicant-induced Loss of Tolerance
https://pdfs.semanticscholar.org/2c25/1e67a77db03b6cd06848554549ad383a30e5.pdf?_ga=2.60651566.2070009590.1539666639-547826459.1530180510Miller, C.S. (2001).

Toxicant-induced loss of tolerance. *Addiction, 96 1*, 115-37.

24) What You Should Know About Lubricant Toxicity
https://www.machinerylubrication.com/Read/30448/know-lubricant-toxicity

25) Formaldehyde in your fabrics
https://oecotextiles.wordpress.com/2011/01/04/formaldehyde-in-your-fabrics/

26) Airbrush, Spray Cans, and Spray Guns
https://ehs.princeton.edu/health-safety-the-campus-community/art-theater-safety/art-safety/painting-and-drawing#ascasg

27) Feeling stressed? Then go mow the lawn, claims research: The sweet smell of freshly cut grass can relieve stress, scientists claim
https://www.telegraph.co.uk/news/science/6094786/Feeling-stressed-Then-go-mow-the-lawn-claims-research.html

28) 13 Health Benefits of Kerson Fruit
https://paulhaider.wordpress.com/2015/03/31/13-health-benefits-of-kerson-fruit/

29) Smells to make you well
https://www.express.co.uk/life-style/health/362320/Smells-to-make-you-well

30) Root Canals are EXTREMELY toxic - Dr. Mercola
https://www.youtube.com/watch?v=Q02mLcdBtGI

31)   The Dangers of Amalgam Fillings
https://draxe.com/dangers-of-amalgam-fillings/

32)   5 things you need to know about chemical hair straightening treatments
https://saludmovil.com/chemical-hair-straightening-treatments-safety/

33)   Medical Management Guidelines for Formaldehyde
https://www.atsdr.cdc.gov/mmg/mmg.asp?id=216&tid=39

34)   Violent Behavior: A Solution in Plain Sight
https://www.westonaprice.org/health-topics/environmental-toxins/violent-behavior-a-solution-in-plain-sight/

35)   Cholesterol: Friend Or Foe?
https://www.westonaprice.org/health-topics/know-your-fats/cholesterol-friend-or-foe/

B. On NIACIN (Vitamin B3)
   1. Nutritional Links to Depression and Mental Illness
       https://www.youtube.com/watch?v=HiI7AcH1UIU
   2. How to Take Niacin (Vitamin B3) for Depression and Anxiety https://www.foodmatters.com/article/how-to-take-niacin-vitamin-b3-for-depression-and-anxiety
   3. Reviews of NIACIN: The Real Story
       http://www.doctoryourself.com/niacinreviews.html
   4. Vitamin B3 for Depression: Case Report and Review of the Literature https://ionhealth.ca/wp-content/uploads/resources/PDFs/Vitamin-B3-for-Depression-Case-Report-and-Review-of-the-Literature-25.3.pdf

5. Vitamin B3: Deficiency Symptoms
http://www.newsmax.com/FastFeatures/health01-Vitamin-B3-Deficiency/2011/02/23/id/387137/
6. Dr. Mercola Interviews Dr. Andrew Saul
https://www.youtube.com/watch?v=8ru6IPFPeTQ

C. On Sunlight, Vitamin D and Depression

1. Suicidal patients are deficient in vitamin D, associated with a pro-inflammatory status in the blood
https://www.ncbi.nlm.nih.gov/pubmed/25240206
2. The association between low vitamin D and depressive disorders https://www.nature.com/articles/mp201336
3. Vitamin D deficiency and depression in adults: systematic review and meta-analysis
https://www.ncbi.nlm.nih.gov/pubmed/23377209
4. Higher serum 25-hydroxy vitamin D concentrations are related to a reduced risk of depression
https://www.ncbi.nlm.nih.gov/pubmed/25989997
5. Vitamin D and Depression: Where is all the Sunshine?
https://www.ncbi.nlm.nih.gov/pmc/articles/PMC2908269/
6. Sunshine and the cardiovascular benefits – a dose of sunshine!
https://www.ncbi.nlm.nih.gov/pmc/articles/PMC5592328/
7. Vitamin D and Cardiovascular Disease
https://www.ncbi.nlm.nih.gov/pmc/articles/PMC3257655/

8. Vitamin D deficiency is associated with low mood and worse cognitive performance in older adults
https://www.ncbi.nlm.nih.gov/pubmed/17138809/

9. Vitamin D deficiency is associated with anxiety and depression in fibromyalgia
https://www.ncbi.nlm.nih.gov/pubmed/16850115/

10. Vitamin D supplementation improves cytokine profiles in patients with congestive heart failure: a double-blind, randomized, placebo-controlled trial
https://www.ncbi.nlm.nih.gov/pubmed/16600924

D. On Saturated Fats and their Vital Importance To Our Mental And Physical Well-Being

1. On Cholesterol and Mental Illnesses

   1) The Implications Of Low Cholesterol In Depression And Suicide
   https://www.greatplainslaboratory.com/articles-1/2015/11/13/the-implications-of-low-cholesterol-in-depression-and-suicide

   2) Low Cholesterol and Its Psychological Effects: Low Cholesterol is Linked to Depression, Suicide, and Violence
   https://www.psychologytoday.com/us/blog/the-breakthrough-depression-solution/201106/low-cholesterol-and-its-psychological-effects

   3) Low Cholesterol and Suicide (Again) Another study links low cholesterol to depression and suicide attempts.

https://www.psychologytoday.com/us/blog/evolutionary-psychiatry/201803/low-cholesterol-and-suicide-again

4) Serum lipid levels and suicidality: a meta-analysis of 65 epidemiological studies
https://www.ncbi.nlm.nih.gov/pmc/articles/PMC4688029/

5) Hypocholesterolemia is an independent risk factor for depression disorder and suicide attempt in Northern Mexican population
https://bmcpsychiatry.biomedcentral.com/articles/10.1186/s12888-018-1596-z

6) Lipids, depression and suicide
https://www.ncbi.nlm.nih.gov/pubmed/12640327

7) Brain membrane lipids in major depression and anxiety disorders
https://www.ncbi.nlm.nih.gov/pubmed/25542508

8) Cholesterol: It's All Good
http://healthimpactnews.com/2012/cholesterol-its-all-good/

9) Effects of nutrients (in food) on the structure and function of the nervous system: update on dietary requirements for brain. Part 2 : macronutrients
https://www.ncbi.nlm.nih.gov/pubmed/17066210

10)   Balut
https://en.wikipedia.org/wiki/Balut_(food)

11)   You're 112% More Likely To Get Depressed If You're Not Eating THIS

https://www.prevention.com/food-nutrition/a20504330/depression-and-fat-consumption/

12) Violent Behavior Linked to Nutritional Deficiencies https://www.westonaprice.org/health-topics/violent-behavior-linked-to-nutritional-defiencies/

13) Violent Behavior: A Solution in Plain Sight https://www.westonaprice.org/health-topics/environmental-toxins/violent-behavior-a-solution-in-plain-sight/

2. On Vegetable Oils And Their Detrimental Effects On Our Health

1) The Great Con-ola https://www.westonaprice.org/health-topics/know-your-fats/the-great-con-ola/

2) Evidence From Randomized Controlled Trials Did Not Support The Introduction Of Dietary Fat Guidelines In 1977 And 1983: A Systematic Review And Meta-Analysis https://openheart.bmj.com/content/2/1/e000196?sid=7217c2a8-513e-4e7e-837a-fe5389053fde

3) The Nutrition Source: Ask The Expert: Concerns About Canola Oil https://www.hsph.harvard.edu/nutritionsource/2015/04/13/ask-the-expert-concerns-about-canola-oil/

4) 8 Ways Canola Oil Is Bad for Brain Health https://bebrainfit.com/canola-oil-bad-brain/

5) Choice of cooking oils--myths and realities
https://www.ncbi.nlm.nih.gov/pubmed/10063298?dopt=Abstract
6) Good Fats, Bad Fats: Separating Fact from Fiction
https://www.westonaprice.org/health-topics/know-your-fats/good-fats-bad-fats-separating-fact-from-fiction/

3. On Beef Fats And Other Animal Products For Physical And Mental Health
1) It's the Beef: Myths & Truths About Beef
https://www.westonaprice.org/health-topics/food-features/its-the-beef/
2) Guts and Grease: The Diet of Native Americans
https://www.westonaprice.org/health-topics/traditional-diets/guts-and-grease-the-diet-of-native-americans/
3) Efficacy of conjugated linoleic acid for reducing fat mass: a meta-analysis in humans
https://academic.oup.com/ajcn/article/85/5/1203/4632999 (Beef fats help us burn fat!)
4) 5 Reasons to Eat Beef Tallow and Easy Beef Tallow Recipe https://www.grassfedgirl.com/grass-fed-beef-tallow-the-cheap-and-easy-fat-burner/
5) Beef tallow increases the potency of conjugated linoleic acid in the reduction of mouse mammary tumor metastasis
https://www.ncbi.nlm.nih.gov/pubmed/16365064 (Shows tallow's benefits against cancer)

6) Conjugated linoleic acid suppresses colon carcinogenesis in azoxymethane-pretreated rats with long-term feeding of diet containing beef tallow https://www.ncbi.nlm.nih.gov/pubmed/20143104 (Shows tallow's benefits against cancer)

7) Beef Fat Prevents Alcoholic Liver Disease in the Rat https://onlinelibrary.wiley.com/doi/abs/10.1111/j.1530-0277.1989.tb00276.x

8) Association between Dietary Patterns and Depressive Symptoms Over Time: A 10-Year Follow-Up Study of the GAZEL Cohort https://www.ncbi.nlm.nih.gov/pmc/articles/PMC3520961/ (This study shows that animal fats helps reduce depressive symptoms)

9) 5 Reasons to Eat Beef Tallow and Easy Beef Tallow Recipe https://www.grassfedgirl.com/grass-fed-beef-tallow-the-cheap-and-easy-fat-burner/

10)	High-fat diet selectively protects against the effects of chronic social stress in the mouse. https://www.ncbi.nlm.nih.gov/pubmed/21742017 (This study shows that animal fats help reduce depressive symptoms)

11)	Dietary fat is not a major determinant of body fat https://www.ncbi.nlm.nih.gov/pubmed/12566139

4. On The Mental and Physical Health Benefits of Saturated Fats: Reasons why we don't need to fear saturated fats. We should appreciate them and indulge in them!

Rose C. Manalo

1) The Pursuit of Happiness: How Nutrient-dense Animal Fats Promote Mental and Emotional Health
https://www.westonaprice.org/health-topics/the-pursuit-of-happiness/

2) Saturated Fat Does a Body Good: Exploring the Biological Roles of These Long-Demonized Yet Heroic Nutrients
https://www.westonaprice.org/health-topics/abcs-of-nutrition/saturated-fat-body-good/

3) Myths & Truths About Vegetarianism
https://www.westonaprice.org/health-topics/vegetarianism-and-plant-foods/myths-of-vegetarianism/

4) Association between Dietary Patterns and Depressive Symptoms Over Time: A 10-Year Follow-Up Study of the GAZEL Cohort
https://www.ncbi.nlm.nih.gov/pmc/articles/PMC3520961/

5) FAQ-Fats and Oils
https://www.westonaprice.org/health-topics/faq-fats-and-oils/

6) Some Recent Studies on Fats
https://www.westonaprice.org/health-topics/know-your-fats/some-recent-studies-on-fats/

7) Save Your Bacon
https://www.westonaprice.org/health-topics/food-features/save-your-bacon/

8) Beyond Cholesterol
https://www.westonaprice.org/health-topics/beyond-cholesterol/

5. On Saturated Fats Not The Cause Of Heart Diseases

1) Study: Saturated Fat Not Associated with Risk of Coronary Artery Disease, Coconut Oil and Dairy Fat Healthy
http://healthimpactnews.com/2013/study-saturated-fat-not-associated-with-risk-of-coronary-artery-disease-coconut-oil-and-dairy-fat-healthy/

2) Big Pharma Study: USDA Dietary Guidelines on Fats are Wrong
http://healthimpactnews.com/2014/big-pharma-study-usda-dietary-guidelines-on-fats-are-wrong/

3) Meta-analysis of prospective cohort studies evaluating the association of saturated fat with cardiovascular disease
https://www.ncbi.nlm.nih.gov/pubmed/20071648?itool=EntrezSystem2.PEntrez.Pubmed.Pubmed_ResultsPanel.Pubmed_RVDocSum&ordinalpos=2

4) Dietary fats and health: dietary recommendations in the context of scientific evidence
https://www.ncbi.nlm.nih.gov/pubmed/23674795

5) What Causes Heart Disease?
https://www.westonaprice.org/health-topics/modern-diseases/what-causes-heart-disease/

6) Taking the Fear Out of Eating Fat
https://www.westonaprice.org/health-

topics/making-it-practical/taking-the-fear-out-of-eating-fat/

7) Association of Dietary, Circulating, and Supplement Fatty Acids With Coronary Risk: A Systematic Review and Meta-analysis https://pdfs.semanticscholar.org/cdd7/b60881b33c880c2764f27c75f0840e6b4163.pdf

E. On Raw Milk and its Benefits on Mental and Physical Health:

1. THE FACTS ABOUT REAL RAW MILK https://www.realmilk.com/
2. Frequently-Asked-Questions-Dairy https://www.westonaprice.org/health-topics/faq-dairy/
3. Benefits Of Raw Milk Range From Help With Allergies To Boosting The Immune System https://www.realmilk.com/many-benefits-raw-milk/
4. Raw Milk Benefits Skin, Allergies and Immunity https://draxe.com/raw-milk-benefits/
5. Health Benefits of Raw Milk https://www.drdeborahmd.com/health-benefits-raw-milk
6. Study: Raw Milk Can Reduce Asthma and Allergies https://articles.mercola.com/sites/articles/archive/2016/02/09/raw-milk-asthma-allergies.aspx
7. Studies Showing Raw (Farm) Milk Protective Against Asthma And Allergies https://www.realmilk.com/health/raw-milk-protective-against-asthma-and-allergies/
8. Inverse Association Of Farm Milk Consumption With Asthma And Allergy In Rural And Suburban Populations

Across Europe
https://www.ncbi.nlm.nih.gov/pubmed/17456213

9. The Protective Effect Of Farm Milk Consumption On Childhood Asthma And Atopy: The GABRIELA Study
https://www.ncbi.nlm.nih.gov/pubmed/21875744

10. How I Reversed My Son's Asthma
https://www.weedemandreap.com/how-i-reversed-my-sons-asthma/

11. https://www.youtube.com/watch?v=HatFVFDdrLQ
"Digestible Dairy" - A Weston A. Price Foundation Talk by Dr. Timothy Weeks of Whole-Body Health (on fermented food like raw milk, yoghurt and kefir)

12. Milk: It Does a Body Good?
https://www.westonaprice.org/health-topics/making-it-practical/milk-it-does-a-body-good/

F. On Salmon and How it Helps with Depression and Anxiety

1. Eating a lot of fish may help curb depression risk -- at least in Europe Association equally significant among men and women, pooled data analysis shows
https://www.sciencedaily.com/releases/2015/09/150910185034.htm

2. Omega-3s Lower Risk of Depression
https://psychcentral.com/news/2007/03/29/omega-3s-lower-risk-of-depression

3. Fish: One of the Best Foods That Help Depression
https://universityhealthnews.com/daily/depression/fish-one-of-the-best-foods-that-help-depression/

4. Fish consumption and risk of depression: a meta-analysis
https://www.ncbi.nlm.nih.gov/pubmed/26359502
5. The efficacy of omega-3 supplementation for major depression: a randomized controlled trial.
http://europepmc.org/abstract/med/20584525
6. Omega-3 Relieves Anxiety, Inflammation in Healthy Sample
https://psychcentral.com/news/2011/07/14/omega-3-relieves-anxiety-inflammation-in-healthy-sample/27749.html
7. What's New and Beneficial about Salmon
http://www.whfoods.com/genpage.php?tname=foodspice&dbid=104
8. Dietary n-3 PUFA, fish consumption and depression: A systematic review and meta-analysis of observational studies
https://www.jad-journal.com/article/S0165-0327(16)30754-6/abstract
9. Prozac of the Sea: Fats that fight depression: Fish of the sea and omega-3s
https://www.psychologytoday.com/us/articles/199605/prozac-the-sea
10. Salmon May Help Relieve Depression
https://www.webmd.com/depression/news/20020315/salmon-may-help-relieve-depression

G. On Gut Health And Its Relevance To Our Mental And Physical Health

1. A randomized controlled trial of dietary improvement for adults with major depression (the 'SMILES' trial)

https://www.ncbi.nlm.nih.gov/pmc/articles/PMC5282719/

2. Relationship Between Diet And Mental Health In Children And Adolescents: A Systematic Review
https://www.ncbi.nlm.nih.gov/pubmed/25208008/

3. These two studies show the effect of good nutrition by mother during pregnancy and by child for the first years of life, on the child's mental health.

   1) Maternal And Early Postnatal Nutrition And Mental Health Of Offspring By Age 5 Years: A Prospective Cohort Study
   https://www.ncbi.nlm.nih.gov/pubmed/24074470/

   2) Maternal Dietary Patterns During Pregnancy And Child Internalizing And Externalizing Problems. The Generation R Study
   https://www.ncbi.nlm.nih.gov/pubmed/23541912/

4. The gut microbiome and diet in psychiatry: focus on depression
https://www.ncbi.nlm.nih.gov/pubmed/25415497/ (This study shows the unmistakable relationship between the gut microbiota and the brain.)

5. The impact of whole-of-diet interventions on depression and anxiety: a systematic review of randomized controlled trials. https://www.ncbi.nlm.nih.gov/pubmed/25465596/ (This study looked into evidence of how diet can affect depression and anxiety.)

6. So, depression is an inflammatory disease, but where does the inflammation come from?

https://www.ncbi.nlm.nih.gov/pubmed/24228900/ (This study explores the possible causes of inflammation that leads to depression. Among those covered are: poor diet, gut permeability, and vitamin D deficiency, all of which were part of my over-all ill health when my depression started.)

7. Understanding Nutrition, Depression And Mental Illnesses https://www.ncbi.nlm.nih.gov/pmc/articles/PMC2738337/ (This article discusses the strong relationship among, well, nutrition, depression and mental illnesses.)

8. Is eating behavior manipulated by the gastrointestinal microbiota? Evolutionary pressures and potential mechanisms https://onlinelibrary.wiley.com/doi/full/10.1002/bies.201400071

9. Overcoming Psychiatric Problems by Healing the Digestive System - Dr. Campbell-McBride https://www.youtube.com/watch?v=u-TupRO7qjc

10. Wise Traditions podcast #63 Heal your gut w/ Hilary Boynton https://www.youtube.com/watch?v=IEn2rkOqChE

11. Inflammatory dietary pattern and risk of depression among women https://www.ncbi.nlm.nih.gov/pubmed/24095894

H. On Bone Broth, Gelatine, Gut Health and Mental Conditions

1. Getting at the Gut: A Solution for Treating Bipolar Disorder https://www.westonaprice.org/health-topics/getting-at-the-gut/

2. Offal of the Week: Beef Tendon
   http://www.eatmedaily.com/2009/09/offal-of-the-week-beef-tendon/

3. Why Broth is Beautiful: Essential Roles for Proline, Glycine and Gelatin reduces inflammation, arthritis and joint pain
   https://www.westonaprice.org/health-topics/why-broth-is-beautiful-essential-roles-for-proline-glycine-and-gelatin/

4. Chicken Soup for a Cold
   https://www.unmc.edu/publicrelations/media/press-kits/chicken-soup/ (heal disorders like allergies, asthma and arthritis by boosting the immune system)

5. Shocking Benefits Of Eating Chicken Feet
   http://www.healthyandsmartliving.com/benefits-eating-chicken-feet/

6. 24-Week study on the use of collagen hydrolysate as a dietary supplement in athletes with activity-related joint pain https://www.ncbi.nlm.nih.gov/pubmed/18416885

7. Gelatin tannate reduces the proinflammatory effects of lipopolysaccharide in human intestinal epithelial cells https://www.ncbi.nlm.nih.gov/pmc/articles/PMC3358810/ (gelatin reduces intestinal inflammation)

8. Serum laminin and collagen IV in inflammatory bowel disease https://www.ncbi.nlm.nih.gov/pubmed/14600124 (proves that a healthy digestive system needs collagen)

9. Oral supplementation of specific collagen peptides has beneficial effects on human skin physiology: a double-blind, placebo-controlled study
   https://www.ncbi.nlm.nih.gov/pubmed/23949208

10. Chicken soup inhibits neutrophil chemotaxis in vitro
    https://www.ncbi.nlm.nih.gov/pubmed/11035691

11. Glycine administration attenuates skeletal muscle wasting in a mouse model of cancer cachexia. https://www.ncbi.nlm.nih.gov/pubmed/23835111 (protects skeletal muscle breakdown)

12. N-Acetylglucosamine for Treatment of Inflammatory Bowel Disease https://www.naturalmedicinejournal.com/journal/2015-04/n-acetylglucosamine-treatment-inflammatory-bowel-disease (Glycosaminoglycans (GAGs) supports a healthy digestive system)

13. Oral ingestion of a hydrolyzed gelatin meal in subjects with normal weight and in obese patients: Postprandial effect on circulating gut peptides, glucose and insulin. https://www.ncbi.nlm.nih.gov/pubmed/18319637 (Helps in obesity by normalizing gut hormones)

14. Leaky Gut, Demystified https://paleoleap.com/leaky-gut-demystified/

15. Meat, Organs, Bones and Skin: Nutrition for Mental Health https://www.westonaprice.org/health-topics/meat-organs-bones-and-skin/

16. Why Broth is Beautiful: Essential Roles for Proline, Glycine and Gelatin https://www.westonaprice.org/health-topics/why-broth-is-beautiful-essential-roles-for-proline-glycine-and-gelatin/

I. On Coconut Oil and its Tremendous Mental and Physical Health Benefits:

1. Study: Virgin Coconut Oil More Effective than Drugs in Combating Stress and Depression

http://coconutoil.com/study-virgin-coconut-oil-more-effective-than-drugs-in-combating-stress-and-depression/

2. Top 10 Evidence-Based Health Benefits of Coconut Oil https://www.healthline.com/nutrition/top-10-evidence-based-health-benefits-of-coconut-oil

3. The Health Benefits of Coconuts & Coconut Oil: Coconuts and coconut oil contain health-promoting saturated fatty acids and derivative compounds which have powerful antimicrobial properties https://pdfs.semanticscholar.org/b829/84c8fb08b5649483 1caf77165379bb941bee.pdf

4. Coconut Oil is Beneficial for Your Heart: Shining the Truth on Mainstream Media's Negative Attacks Against Coconut Oil http://healthimpactnews.com/2014/coconut-oil-is-beneficial-for-your-heart-shining-the-truth-on-mainstream-medias-negative-attacks-against-coconut-oil/

5. In the Land of Oz: The Latest Attack on Coconut Oil https://www.westonaprice.org/health-topics/know-your-fats/in-the-land-of-oz-the-latest-attack-on-coconut-oil/

6. How Coconut Oil Can Help You Lose Weight and Belly Fat https://www.healthline.com/nutrition/coconut-oil-and-weight-loss#section1

7. A diet rich in coconut oil reduces diurnal postprandial variations in circulating tissue plasminogen activator antigen and fasting lipoprotein (a) compared with a diet rich in unsaturated fat in women https://www.ncbi.nlm.nih.gov/pubmed/14608053

8. Angiogenic and wound healing potency of fermented virgin coconut oil: in vitro and in vivo studies

https://www.ncbi.nlm.nih.gov/pubmed/29218091?dopt=Abstract

9. Anti-inflammatory, analgesic, and antipyretic activities of virgin coconut oil.
https://www.ncbi.nlm.nih.gov/pubmed/20645831

10. Coconut Oil: Non-Alternative Drug Treatment Against Alzheimer's Disease
https://www.ncbi.nlm.nih.gov/pubmed/26667739?dopt=Abstract

11. Medium chain triglycerides (MCT) in aging and arteriosclerosis
https://www.ncbi.nlm.nih.gov/pubmed/3519928

12. Virgin coconut oil (VCO) by normalizing NLRP3 inflammasome showed potential neuroprotective effects in Amyloid-β induced toxicity and high-fat diet fed rat
https://www.ncbi.nlm.nih.gov/pubmed/29729307?dopt=Abstract

13. Dietary Supplementation with Virgin Coconut Oil Improves Lipid Profile and Hepatic Antioxidant Status and Has Potential Benefits on Cardiovascular Risk Indices in Normal Rats
https://www.ncbi.nlm.nih.gov/pubmed/28816548?dopt=Abstract

14. Virgin coconut oil maintains redox status and improves glycemic conditions in high fructose fed rats
https://www.ncbi.nlm.nih.gov/pubmed/26788013

15. Effect of virgin coconut oil enriched diet on the antioxidant status and paraoxonase 1 activity in ameliorating the oxidative stress in rats - a comparative study
https://www.ncbi.nlm.nih.gov/pubmed/23892389

16. An ecological study for Sri Lanka about health effects of coconut
https://www.ncbi.nlm.nih.gov/pubmed/26520863?dopt=Abstract

17. Coconut oil attenuates the effects of amyloid-β on cortical neurons in vitro
https://www.ncbi.nlm.nih.gov/pubmed/24150106?dopt=Abstract

18. Dietary fatty acids and oxidative stress in the heart mitochondria
https://www.ncbi.nlm.nih.gov/pubmed/20691812

19. Philippine Journal Of CARDIOLOGY: COCONUT OIL: Atherogenic or Not? (What therefore causes Atherosclerosis?)
http://www.coconutoil.com/DayritCardiology.pdf

20. Cholesterol, coconuts, and diet on Polynesian atolls: a natural experiment: the Pukapuka and Tokelau island studies
https://www.ncbi.nlm.nih.gov/pubmed/7270479?dopt=Abstract

21. The role of coconut and coconut oil in coronary heart disease in Kerala, south India
https://www.ncbi.nlm.nih.gov/pubmed/9316363?dopt=Abstract

22. What Type of Coconut Oil is Best? How to Choose a Coconut Oil http://coconutoil.com/what-type-of-coconut-oil-is-best-how-to-choose-a-coconut-oil/

23. Protective effects of medium-chain triglycerides on the liver and gut in rats administered endotoxin

https://www.ncbi.nlm.nih.gov/pubmed/12560783?dopt=
Abstract

J.   On Ketogenic Diet and Depression:

1.   How the ketogenic lifestyle reversed my depression
     https://www.ketovangelist.com/how-the-ketogenic-
     lifestyle-reversed-my-depression/
2.   The High-fat Ketogenic Diet for Cognitive Health: Proven
     Remedies for the Alzheimer's Epidemic
     http://coconutoil.com/the-high-fat-ketogenic-diet-for-
     cognitive-health-proven-remedies-for-the-alzheimers-
     epidemic/
3.   Gestational ketogenic diet programs brain structure and
     susceptibility to depression & anxiety in the adult mouse
     offspring
     https://www.ncbi.nlm.nih.gov/pmc/articles/PMC4309881
     /
4.   The fiery landscape of depression: A review of the
     inflammatory hypothesis
     https://www.ncbi.nlm.nih.gov/pmc/articles/PMC3809277
     /
5.   The antidepressant properties of the ketogenic diet
     https://www.biologicalpsychiatryjournal.com/article/S000
     6-3223(04)01006-6/fulltext
6.   Ketogenic Diets for Psychiatric Disorders: A New 2017
     Review: Where the science stands, and what it means for
     you
     https://www.psychologytoday.com/us/blog/diagnosis-

diet/201706/ketogenic-diets-psychiatric-disorders-new-2017-review

7. Depression Treatment https://www.ketogenic-diet-resource.com/depression-treatment.html

8. The Ketogenic Diet and Depression https://thenoakesfoundation.org/news/blog/the-ketogenic-diet-and-depression

K. On Breastfeeding and Mental and Physical Health

1. "Effect Of Breast And Formula Feeding On Gut Microbiota Shaping In Newborns"Https://Www.Ncbi.Nlm.Nih.Gov/Pmc/Articles/PMC3472256/

2. Fat And Cholesterol In Human Milk Https://Www.Westonaprice.Org/Health-Topics/Childrens-Health/Fat-And-Cholesterol-In-Human-Milk/

3. Breastfeeding And Mental Health Http://Waba.Org.My/Breastfeeding-And-Mental-Health/

4. Successful Breastfeeding …And Successful Alternatives Https://Www.Westonaprice.Org/Health-Topics/Childrens-Health/Successful-Breastfeeding-And-Successful-Alternatives/

5. Is Mother's Milk Sterile? Recent Research On Human Milk Https://Www.Westonaprice.Org/Health-Topics/Childrens-Health/Is-Mothers-Milk-Sterile-Recent-Research-On-Human-Milk/

6. Nourishing A Growing Baby
   Https://Www.Westonaprice.Org/Health-Topics/Childrens-Health/Nourishing-A-Growing-Baby/
7. Vitamin D In The Infant: Requirements For Safety
   Https://Www.Westonaprice.Org/Health-Topics/Childrens-Health/Vitamin-D-In-The-Infant-Requirements-For-Safety/
8. The Motherhood Diet
   Https://Www.Westonaprice.Org/Podcast/55-The-Motherhood-Diet/
9. More Government Promotion Of Soy-Based Infant Formulas Https://Www.Westonaprice.Org/Health-Topics/Soy-Alert/More-Government-Promotion-Of-Soy-Based-Infant-Formulas-2/
10. How To Have The Healthiest Babies (Principle #11) With Sally Fallon Morell
    Https://Www.Westonaprice.Org/Podcast/142-How-To-Have-The-Healthiest-Babies-Principle-11/
11. Calming The Cry Of Colic
    Https://Www.Westonaprice.Org/Health-Topics/Childrens-Health/Calming-The-Cry-Of-Colic/
12. Vitamins For Fetal Development: Conception To Birth
    Https://Www.Westonaprice.Org/Health-Topics/Childrens-Health/Vitamins-For-Fetal-Development-Conception-To-Birth/
13. The Long-Term Effects Of Breastfeeding On Child And Adolescent Mental Health: A Pregnancy Cohort Study Followed For 14 Years.
    Https://Www.Ncbi.Nlm.Nih.Gov/Pubmed/20004910

14. MENTAL HEALTH AND EMOTIONAL DEVELOPMENT: These Studies Look At The Effects Of Breastfeeding On Children's Mental Health, Behavior And Emotional Development Https://Www.Unicef.Org.Uk/Babyfriendly/News-And-Research/Baby-Friendly-Research/Infant-Health-Research/Infant-Health-Research-Mental-Health-And-Emotional-Development/

15. THE LANCET: INCREASING BREASTFEEDING WORLDWIDE COULD PREVENT OVER 800,000 CHILD DEATHS EVERY YEAR: Failing To Breastfeed Costs The Global Economy Around US$302 Billion Every Year Https://Www.Unicef.Org.Uk/Babyfriendly/Lancet-Increasing-Breastfeeding-Worldwide-Prevent-800000-Child-Deaths-Every-Year/

16. THE IMPACT OF BREASTFEEDING ON MATERNAL AND CHILD HEALTH ACTA PAEDIATRICA SPECIAL ISSUE Https://Www.Unicef.Org.Uk/Babyfriendly/News-And-Research/Baby-Friendly-Research/Infant-Health-Research/Infant-Health-Research-Meta-Analyses/The-Impact-Of-Breastfeeding-On-Maternal-And-Child-Health/

17. The Link Between Breastfeeding And Mental Health Http://Theattachedfamily.Com/Membersonly/?P=2774

L. On Avocados And Its Protective Benefits For Mental And Physical Health

1. Effect of a moderate fat diet with and without avocados on lipoprotein particle number, size and subclasses in overweight and obese adults: a randomized, controlled trial https://www.ncbi.nlm.nih.gov/pubmed/25567051

2. Impact of avocado-enriched diets on plasma lipoproteins: A meta-analysis. https://www.ncbi.nlm.nih.gov/pubmed/26892133

3. A randomized 3×3 crossover study to evaluate the effect of Hass avocado intake on post-ingestive satiety, glucose and insulin levels, and subsequent energy intake in overweight adults https://www.ncbi.nlm.nih.gov/pubmed/24279738

4. Effects of Avocado (Persea americana) on Metabolic Syndrome: A Comprehensive Systematic Review https://onlinelibrary.wiley.com/doi/abs/10.1002/ptr.5805

5. Inhibition of prostate cancer cell growth by an avocado extract: role of lipid-soluble bioactive substances https://www.sciencedirect.com/science/article/pii/S0955286304001597

6. Hass avocado composition and potential health effects https://www.ncbi.nlm.nih.gov/pubmed/23638933

7. Avocado consumption is associated with better diet quality and nutrient intake, and lower metabolic syndrome risk in US adults: results from the National Health and Nutrition Examination Survey (NHANES) 2001-2008 https://www.ncbi.nlm.nih.gov/pubmed/23282226

8. Effect of an avocado oil-enhanced diet (Persea americana) on sucrose-induced insulin resistance in Wistar rats
   https://www.ncbi.nlm.nih.gov/pubmed/28911589

M. On Monosodium Glutamate And Its Detrimental Effects On Physical And Mental Health:

1. New Propaganda About MSG
   https://www.westonaprice.org/health-topics/modern-foods/new-propaganda-about-msg/
2. Baby Formula: MSG, Excitatory Neurotoxins & HFCS
   http://www.eatingdisorderpro.com/2011/01/26/baby-formula-msg-excitatory-neurotoxins-hfcs/
3. MSG: Is This Silent Killer Lurking in Your Kitchen Cabinets
   https://articles.mercola.com/sites/articles/archive/2009/04/21/msg-is-this-silent-killer-lurking-in-your-kitchen-cabinets.aspx
4. Top 7 MSG Side Effects + 15 Foods with MSG to Avoid
   https://draxe.com/msg/
5. Interview With Jodi Ledley, the author of "Adventures with Jodi: How One Girl Stopped Migraines and Chronic Pain and Accidently Improved Her Family's Health!"
   https://www.westonaprice.org/health-topics/interview-with-jodi-ledley/
6. The monosodium glutamate symptom complex: assessment in a double-blind, placebo-controlled, randomized study
   https://www.ncbi.nlm.nih.gov/pubmed/9215242?dopt=Abstract

7. MSG in Infant Formula
   https://www.westonaprice.org/health-topics/modern-foods/msg-in-infant-formula/
8. Adverse Effects of Monosodium Glutamate on Liver and Kidney Functions in Adult Rats and Potential Protective Effect of Vitamins C and E
   https://pdfs.semanticscholar.org/d7b4/ef522134a89c6db21c7c06607b12c959d5f9.pdf
9. Effect of vitamin E on monosodium glutamate induced hepatotoxicity and oxidative stress in rats
   https://www.ncbi.nlm.nih.gov/pubmed/16955747?dopt=Abstract
10. Monosodium glutamate neonatal treatment as a seizure and excitotoxic model
    https://www.ncbi.nlm.nih.gov/pubmed/20043888?dopt=Abstract
11. Umami and appetite: effects of monosodium glutamate on hunger and food intake in human subjects
    https://www.ncbi.nlm.nih.gov/pubmed/2087510?dopt=Abstract
12. Acquired flavor acceptance and intake facilitated by monosodium glutamate in humans
    https://www.ncbi.nlm.nih.gov/pubmed/18279899?dopt=Abstract
13. Association of monosodium glutamate intake with overweight in Chinese adults: the INTERMAP Study.https://www.ncbi.nlm.nih.gov/pubmed/18497735?dopt=Abstract
14. Obesity, voracity, and short stature: the impact of glutamate on the regulation of appetite

https://www.ncbi.nlm.nih.gov/pubmed/16132059?dopt=
Abstract

N. On Plant Foods, Short-Chain Fatty Acids and Gut Health

1. Nutritional and Medicinal Qualities of Sweet
    potato Tops and Leaves (Cooperative Extension Program
    University of Arkansas at Pine Bluff)
    https://www.uaex.edu/publications/PDF/FSA-6135.pdf

2. Water Spinach, Ipomoea aquatica (Convolvulaceae),
    Ameliorates Lead Toxicity by Inhibiting Oxidative Stress
    and Apoptosis
    https://www.ncbi.nlm.nih.gov/pmc/articles/PMC4608788
    /

3. Astonishing Health Benefits of Water Spinach
    https://healthcautions.com/astonishing-health-benefits-of-
    water-spinach/

4. Kangkong (water spinach) nutrition facts
    https://www.nutrition-and-you.com/kangkong.html

5. SCFA – Gut bacteria's ally in taming autoimmunity and
    inflammation https://drknews.com/scfa-gut-bacteria-ally-
    taming-autoimmunity-inflammation/

6. Are Short Chain Fatty Acids in Gut Microbiota Defensive
    Players for Inflammation and Atherosclerosis?
    https://www.ncbi.nlm.nih.gov/pmc/articles/PMC5517538
    /

7. Formation of short chain fatty acids by the gut microbiota
    and their impact on human metabolism
    https://www.ncbi.nlm.nih.gov/pmc/articles/PMC4939913
    /

8. Resistant Starch: Promise for Improving Human Health
https://www.ncbi.nlm.nih.gov/pmc/articles/PMC3823506/

9. Resistant Starch Produces Short-Chain Fatty Acids Which Benefits the Large Intestine
https://biofoundations.org/resistant-starch-produces-short-chain-fatty-acids-which-benefits-the-large-intestine/

10. How Short-Chain Fatty Acids Affect Health and Weight
https://www.healthline.com/nutrition/short-chain-fatty-acids-101

11. 4 Healthy Reasons to Eat Cooked Green Bananas
http://rise4you.com/2018/05/4-healthy-reasons-to-eat-cooked-green-bananas/

O. On Effects of Nature on our Mental and Physical Health

1. Tree and forest effects on air quality and human health in the United States
https://www.fs.fed.us/nrs/pubs/jrnl/2014/nrs_2014_nowak_001.pdf

2. When Trees Die, People Die
https://www.theatlantic.com/health/archive/2013/01/when-trees-die-people-die/267322/

3. The Relationship Between Trees and Human Health
https://www.ajpmonline.org/article/S0749-3797(12)00804-5/fulltext

4. An Environmental Intervention to Restore Attention in Women With Newly Diagnosed Breast Cancer
https://journals.lww.com/cancernursingonline/Abstract/2

003/08000/An_Environmental_Intervention_to_Restore_ Attention.5.aspx

5. The Health Benefits of Trees
https://www.theatlantic.com/health/archive/2014/07/tre es-good/375129/

6. Green Spaces Make Kids Smarter: A new study finds that vegetation around schools cuts down on air pollution and boosts memory and attention
https://www.theatlantic.com/health/archive/2015/06/gre en-spaces-make-kids-smarter/395924/.

P.   On Squash and Watermelon seeds and their Health Benefits:

1. Protein source tryptophan versus pharmaceutical grade tryptophan as an efficacious treatment for chronic insomnia.
https://www.ncbi.nlm.nih.gov/pubmed/16053244

2. What are the health benefits of pumpkin seeds?
https://www.medicalnewstoday.com/articles/303864.php

3. What's New and Beneficial About Pumpkin seeds
http://www.whfoods.com/genpage.php?tname=foodspice &dbid=82#healthbenefits

4. Top 11 Science-Based Health Benefits of Pumpkin Seeds
https://www.healthline.com/nutrition/11-benefits-of- pumpkin-seeds

5. The Amazing Health Benefits of Watermelon Seeds
http://www.helpmnsave.org/amazing-health-benefits-of- watermelon-seeds/

6. Watermelon Seeds as Food: Nutrient Composition, Phytochemicals and Antioxidant Activity

http://article.sciencepublishinggroup.com/html/10.11648.j
.ijnfs.20160502.18.html#paper-content-4

7. A Comprehensive Review On Watermelon Seed
http://www.journalcra.com/sites/default/files/16829.pdf

Q. WEBSITES

1. About the Weston A. Price Foundation
https://www.westonaprice.org/

2. GAPS Diet http://www.gapsdiet.com/

R. OTHER LINKS

1. How Food Affects Your Mood / Improve Anxiety,
Depression & ADD
https://www.youtube.com/watch?v=9MpeSudXyRs

2. The Gut–Heart Connection
https://kresserinstitute.com/gut-heart-connection/

3. On the Trail of the Elusive X-Factor: A Sixty-Two-Year-
Old Mystery Finally Solved
https://www.westonaprice.org/health-topics/abcs-of-
nutrition/on-the-trail-of-the-elusive-x-factor-a-sixty-two-
year-old-mystery-finally-solved/#heart

4. Vitamin K2: The Top 5 Benefits of a Missing Link to
Health
http://www.nutritionbreakthroughs.com/blog/tag/take-
vitamin-k2-with-fat/

5. 9 Startling Nutrient Deficiencies That Can Cause
Depression https://bipolar1blog.com/2016/12/11/9-
startling-nutrient-deficiencies-that-can-cause-depression/

To Help You Grow in Your Christian Faith

1. Joyce Meyer Ministries
   1) Website: https://www.joycemeyer.org/todaysshow
   2) YouTube Channel:
      https://www.youtube.com/user/joycemeyerministries
2. Charles Stanley In Touch Ministries
   1) Website: https://www.intouch.org/
   2) YouTube Channel:
      https://www.youtube.com/user/InTouchMinistries
3. Joseph Prince Ministries
   1) Website: https://www.josephprince.org/
   2) YouTube Channel:
      https://www.youtube.com/channel/UCJRSBsjLPipnu8y03
      qa2_Iw
4. Biblegateway.com https://www.biblegateway.com/

CHAPTER 12: DIAGRAMS AND GALLERY

Diagram 1: Raw Milk

HEALTH CONDITIONS (PHYSICAL & MENTAL)	PREFERENCES AND CRAVINGS THAT LED TO HEALING	BENEFITS
• compromised immune system • nutritionally deficient • skin allergies • asthma • high blood pressure • insomnia • weakness in limbs • **severe depression and anxiety**	ORGANIC RAW MILK →	• loaded with probiotics that help regulate the gut • boosts and repairs a compromised immune system • reduces and heals allergies like psoriasis, eczema • prevents respiratory diseases such as asthma • a loaded source of vitamins and minerals • helps in balancing hormones • DEPRESSION CURE?

Diagram 2 : Salmon

HEALTH CONDITIONS (PHYSICAL & MENTAL)	PREFERENCES AND CRAVINGS THAT LED TO HEALING	BENEFITS
• Gut Dysbiosis further worsened by • Nutritional Deficiency that led to • Compromised Immune System that led to • Inflammation that led to • Severe Depression and Anxiety	**Salmon** Beef Fats, "Balot", Chicken Skin, Pork Skin/Fat Avocado Coconut Oil/Meat/Water Leafy Greens "Kangkong, Talbos Ng Kamote, Petchay" (Water Spinach, Cabbage, Sweet Potato Tops) Beef Tendons, Chicken Feet, "Buto ng Pakwan at Kalabasa" (Watermelon and Squash Seeds)	• Prevents and heals depression • Provides mood stability • Regulates blood pressure • Protects and regenerates brain cell membranes • Eases and heals digestive and heart inflammation • Relieves skin disorders • Strengthens joints and bones • Prevents cancer • Protects and regenerates the nervous system

Diagram 3: Beef Fats, "Balot", Chicken Skin, Pork Skin/Fat

HEALTH CONDITIONS (PHYSICAL & MENTAL)	PREFERENCES AND CRAVINGS THAT LED TO HEALING	BENEFITS
• Gut Dysbiosis further worsened by ⬇ • Nutritional Deficiency that led to ⬇ • Compromised Immune System that led to ⬇ • Inflammation that led to ⬇ • Severe Depression and Anxiety	Salmon **Beef Fats, "Balot", Chicken Skin, Pork Skin/Fat** Avocado Coconut Oil/Meat/Water Leafy Greens "Kangkong, Talbos Ng Kamote, Petchay" (Water Spinach, Cabbage, Sweet Potato Tops) Beef Tendons, Chicken Feet, "Buto ng Pakwan at Kalabasa" (Watermelon and Squash Seeds)	• Necessary for immune function • Building blocks for hormones • Protection against chronic stress • Helps the body absorb vitamins A, D, E, and K • Essential to build cell membranes especially in the brain • Eases inflammation • Protects the nervous system • Prevents depression and heals depression • Mood stability • skin repair and regeneration • Essential in metabolism • Prevents asthma • Anti-microbial • Helps detoxify the liver

Diagram 4 : Avocado

HEALTH CONDITIONS (PHYSICAL & MENTAL)	PREFERENCES AND CRAVINGS THAT LED TO HEALING	BENEFITS
• Gut Dysbiosis	Salmon	• rich in tryptophan, a vital raw material for the production of serotonin, our brain's feel-good chemical. • loaded with folate and Omega 3 which help in producing hormones and neurotransmitters
further worsened by	Beef Fats, "Balot", Chicken Skin, Pork Skin/Fat	
• Nutritional Deficiency		
that led to	Avocado	
• Compromised Immune System		
that led to	Coconut Oil/Meat/Water	• rich in glutathione which fights inflammation and boosts the immune system • regulates cholesterol and blood glucose levels • very good source of electrolytes that regulate blood pressure • An excellent detoxifier • Helps prevent metabolic syndrome diseases • Has strong antioxidant and neuroprotective properties
• Inflammation		
that led to	Leafy Greens "Kangkong, Talbos Ng Kamote, Petchay" (Water Spinach, Cabbage, Sweet Potato Tops)	
• Severe Depression and Anxiety	Beef Tendons, Chicken Feet, "Buto ng Pakwan at Kalabasa" (Watermelon and Squash Seeds)	

Diagram 5: Coconut Oil/Meat/Water

HEALTH CONDITIONS (PHYSICAL & MENTAL)	PREFERENCES AND CRAVINGS THAT LED TO HEALING	BENEFITS
• Gut Dysbiosis further worsened by • Nutritional Deficiency that led to • Compromised Immune System that led to • Inflammation that led to • Severe Depression and Anxiety	Salmon	• Anti-stress • anti-inflammatory
	Beef Fats, "Balot", Chicken Skin, Pork Skin/Fat	• boosts mood • powerful anti-microbial and anti-virus
	Avocado	• enhances the immune system
	Coconut Oil/Meat/Water	
	Leafy Greens "Kangkong, Talbos Ng Kamote, Petchay" (Water Spinach, Cabbage, Sweet Potato Tops)	• heals a damaged gut • improves metabolism • helps repair brain cells • proven to reverse Alzheimer's
	Beef Tendons, Chicken Feet, "Buto ng Pakwan at Kalabasa" (Watermelon and Squash Seeds)	• reverses Parkinson's disease

Diagram 6: Leafy Greens "Kangkong, Talbos Ng Kamote, Petchay" (Water Spinach, Cabbage, Sweet Potato Tops)

HEALTH CONDITIONS (PHYSICAL & MENTAL)	PREFERENCES AND CRAVINGS THAT LED TO HEALING	BENEFITS
• Gut Dysbiosis further worsened by • Nutritional Deficiency that led to • Compromised Immune System that led to • Inflammation that led to • Severe Depression and Anxiety	Salmon	• Superior than spinach, broccoli, cabbage • These greens, most especially the sweet potato tops are rich in: calcium, iron, vitamins A, C, K, and E • Anti-inflammation • Regulates blood pressure • Anti-cancer • Antimicrobial • Anti-diabetic • Antioxidative activity • Promotes good bowel movement • Anti-diabetic
	Beef Fats, "Balot", Chicken Skin, Pork Skin/Fat	
	Avocado	
	Coconut Oil/Meat/Water	
	Leafy Greens "Kangkong, Talbos Ng Kamote, Petchay" (Water Spinach, Cabbage, Sweet Potato Tops)	
	Beef Tendons, Chicken Feet, "Buto ng Pakwan at Kalabasa" (Watermelon and Squash Seeds)	

Diagram 7: Beef Tendons, Chicken Feet, "Buto ng Pakwan at Kalabasa" (Watermelon and Squash Seeds)

HEALTH CONDITIONS (PHYSICAL & MENTAL)	PREFERENCES AND CRAVINGS THAT LED TO HEALING	BENEFITS
• Gut Dysbiosis *further worsened by*	Salmon	• helps with neurotransmitter signaling and maintenance • helps in nerve cell regeneration • plays a key role in muscle movement esp. the heart • Eases and heals digestive inflammation (leaky gut) • help decrease inflammation in the body
• Nutritional Deficiency *that led to*	Beef Fats, "Balot", Chicken Skin, Pork Skin/Fat	
• Compromised Immune System *that led to*	Avocado	
• Inflammation	Coconut Oil/Meat/Water	
that led to	Leafy Greens "Kangkong, Talbos Ng Kamote, Petchay" (Water Spinach, Cabbage, Sweet Potato Tops)	
• Severe Depression and Anxiety	Beef Tendons, Chicken Feet, "Buto ng Pakwan at Kalabasa" (Watermelon and Squash Seeds)	

Diagram 8: Pre-Gestational

STAGE	INFLUENCING FACTORS	MANIFESTATIONS ON HEALTH
1 PRE-GESTATIONAL	**FATHER:** • Unhealthy sperm due to alcoholism, heavy smoking and poor diet/nutrition • (also, could my father's philandering affected the quality of his seminal fluid?) **MOTHER:** Constant stresses: • physical: caring for 7 prior children • mental: finances and future • emotional: having an unfaithful husband Poor diet: under and malnutrition	FETAL PROGRAMMING?

Diagram 9: Gestational

STAGE	INFLUENCING FACTORS	MANIFESTATIONS ON HEALTH
2 GESTATIONAL	**MOTHER** **Constant stresses:** • physical: caring for 7 prior children • mental: finances and future • emotional: having an unfaithful husband **Poor diet:** • high-sugar diet (fruit-salad iced candies) • low micro nutrients • low fiber	**ON MOTHER:** • weight gain; • gestational diabetes which led to full diabetes • depression and reclusiveness **ON FETUS:** • fetal macrosomia (my birthweight was 9.8 lbs) • Hypo-glycemia

Diagram 10: Birth and Early Feeding

STAGE	INFLUENCING FACTORS	MANIFESTATIONS ON HEALTH
3 BIRTH and EARLY FEEDING	**MANNER OF DELIVERY:** **CAESARIAN** • I did not have the chance to ingest my mother's vaginal/birth canal flora to populate my sterile gut that would have provided me with much-needed beneficial bacteria for a strong immune system. • "vaginal swab" was yet an unknown principle, something I would have benefitted from in lieu of vaginal birth. • I was also not given sufficient skin to skin contact with my mother as proven by the presence of a ready nurse and nanny even before my birth. Mama always had very low pain tolerance. I was told that the nurse was taken under her employ as soon as it was confirmed that mama was to deliver me via caesarian, anticipating that she would be in a lot of pain after surgery. Her incision was 8 inches in length which ran vertically right under her navel, far from the tiny "bikini" incisions popular today. **EARLY FEEDING** • Although my mother, now 88 years old, cannot remember whether she had breast fed me and for how long, I tend to think pessimistically since studies show that mothers who delivered via CS have much less success at breastfeeding. Also, once again, the convenient presence of a nurse and a nanny at mama's employ make the possibility that I was breastfed seem unlikely. When I breastfed my own two sons, I was in a lot of pain from my stitches that extended past my anus. But I didn't have much choice as I had no nanny to call on to each time I was uncomfortable. I just had to find an easier position for me and my son as I breastfed him. This situation is almost unthinkable for Mama who screams at the slightest pain. Hence, it was very unlikely that Mama, having 2 caregivers around to care for me, would endure the pain to breastfeed me. • Babies born via CS tend to be lethargic and not as aggressive as those born vaginally. This, and the fact that the milk of a mother who's under CS anesthesia tend to flow weakly compared to that who delivered vaginally, may mean that it was also likely that I did not benefit from mama's colostrum. • I was told that I latched on to my formula bottle as soon as I was introduced to it. I was on formula from birth all the way to age 8, even preferring it for my snack in school.	Being born via caesarian, a macrosomic baby, and one that didnt enjoy being fed with mother's milk had predisposed me to have a weak microbiota that failed to boost my immune system which eventually set the stage for a host of physical and mental conditions I had very little protection from.

121

Rose C. Manalo

Diagram 11: Early Childhood to Adulthood

STAGE	INFLUENCING FACTORS	MANIFESTATIONS ON HEALTH
4 EARLY CHILDHOOD TO ADULTHOOD	**NUTRITIONAL DEFICIENCIES** • very limited food preferences that favored high simple sugar diet e.g. white rice, candies, desserts • very low fiber and polysaccharides • very low amount of nutritional supplements **EXPOSURE TO TOXINS AND POLLUTANTS** • Insults from vaccinations • repeated antibiotic treatments from childhood to adulthood • root canal procedures • amalgam/mercury cavity fillings • exposure to formaldehyde and other fabric/clothing toxins • exposure to pollutants such as motor vehicle exhausts, home pesticides, hair salon chemicals	• hypoglycemia (low blood sugar) • constant nausea • frequent headaches • frequent diarrhea alternating with constipation • increasing desire for isolation by early teens • irrational fears (of the dark and of objects, e.g. Papa's stuffed animals) • difficulty to maintain ideal weight • skin allergies that come and go (mostly on my legs) • allergic rhinitis that progressed to asthma • hypothyroidism which eventually developed cancer • unwillingness to make new acquaintances • unwillingness to join social gatherings • rage • intense feelings of jealousy • **depression and intense anxiety**

122

Gallery

Note: These are all our personal/family photos

On Beef Tallow:

Beef suet fresh from the market. I wait for these to thaw and then I cut them up into small pieces.

The cut-up beef suet pieces are slowly rendered in their own fats.

You are rewarded with the most amazing beef cracklings. You can sprinkle salt, pepper and cayenne before eating. Best eaten while warm.

Our tubs of beef tallow (rendered beef suet). We use the tallow for anything fried. This amount of tallow will last for 3 to 4 months.

The tallow when used for frying is clear; doesn't smoke easily; and has the nicest, mild beefy aroma. We use it for frying eggs, sautéing and deep frying.

Onions sautéing in tallow. I will use the same fats to fry the fish.
Tallow lends itself to repeated reusing without going dark or oxygenated.
Seldom that I needed to throw a heavily-reused tallow.

These dishes were all cooked in and with tallow.

On Sinigang na Salmon:

As my gut transitioned from inflammation to healing, it needed the raw materials for its process of repair – one of those is Omega 3. Salmon was one of the very first nutritious foods I intensely craved for during this period. Sinigang na Salmon was the perfect vehicle for me to enjoy this fat-laden fish in huge quantities

.

Grilled salmon is another terrific way to enjoy this healing fish. Even my mother loves it. Studies show that Alzheimer patients are deficient in omega 3.

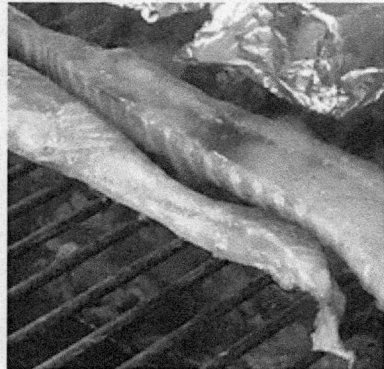

On Bone Broth

We give a lot of credit to bone broth for: healing the lining of our leaky-gut; for healing my husband's knees and elbow joints; and for healing my and Jetross' asthma. When we were on ketogenic diet, it was bone broth that helped us stay satiated and nourished.

To maximize our bone broth, I add pieces of beef tendons. When my son Jetross was having knee joint pains, I prepared small containers of soft beef tendons for quick and easy heating and consumption. These beef tendons worked like magic in repairing our joints.

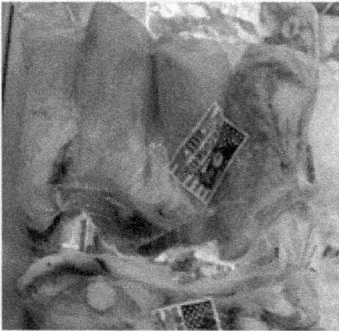

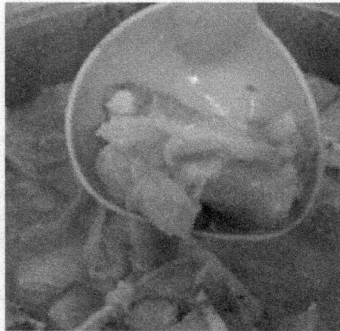

Bone broth can be used as a versatile base for a lot of other soupy dishes. One of our favorites is *Tinolang Manok*. It's a mild yet tasty chicken viand with lots of green papaya, malungay leaves and ginger slices.

Rose C. Manalo

On Balut and Organ Meat: Eating from Nose to Tail

I love to eat *Balot/Balut* right from the shell. To make this traditional Filipino street food into a proper dinner dish, all we need to do is peel a dozen or two of *balut* and sauté these in lots of garlic and creamy butter.

With cravings for Balut, I felt strong cravings for organ meats as well. My favorite ones are barbequed *Tenga ng Baboy* (pork ears) and *Isaw* (pork intestines). Here in the Philippines, you'd be hard-pressed to find a block of streets without someone selling barbequed organ meats like these chicken intestines, head, blood, etc. We are also proficient in cooking dishes with organ meats and the rest of the less popular parts of the animal such as kidney, heart, pig's ears, tail, skin, and liver

Rose C. Manalo

Ears, heart and intestines.

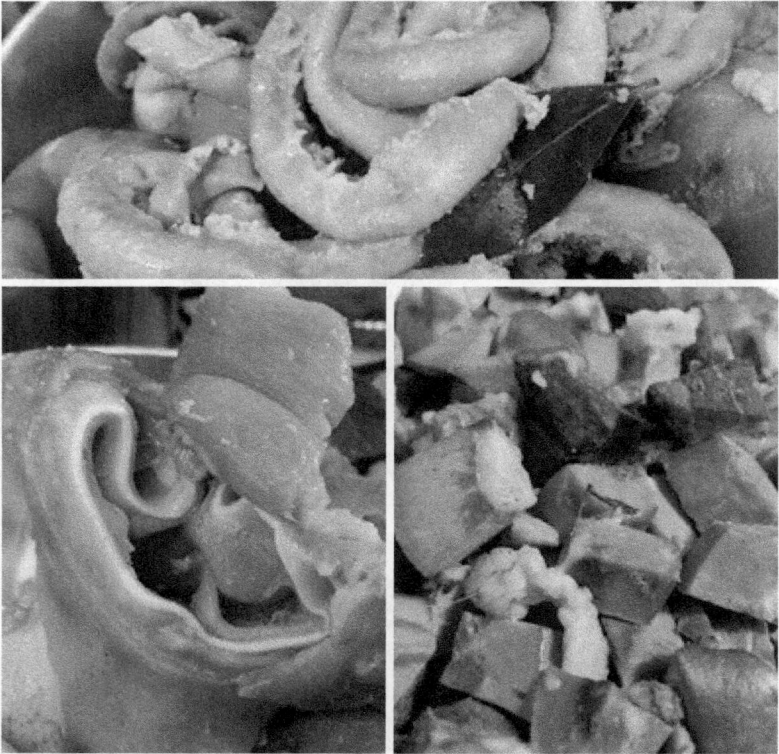

Blood, skin, and tripe.

The gelatin from beef skin helped a lot in reproducing my gut's damaged lining.

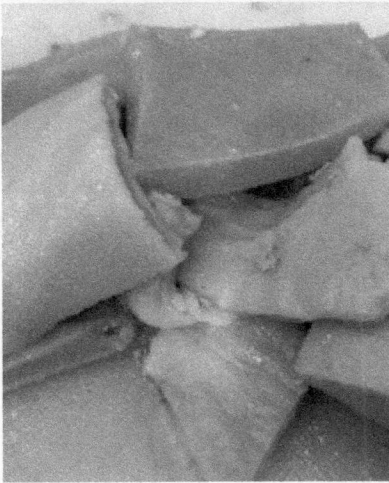

On Raw Milk, Fermented Beverages and Juicing

My seemingly "insane" cravings for raw milk didn't let up until the day that I finally succumbed to it and let myself indulge in liters and liters of fresh, raw carabao and cow milk (sometimes, goat). We also fermented with mother kefir which we divided up into 4 to 6 liters of raw milk which we fermented in less than 24 hours. These kefir-fermented raw milk have healed me over and over from diarrhea

Recently, I was introduced to the taste of *Kombucha* which I am liking too much these days. My sister-in-law Ate Mian is such an apt student of my sister, Ate Se in New York who taught her how to make this delicious fermented gut-health-promoter beverage.

We were on strict ketogenic diet for a full month in 2017. We followed it up with daily juicing for also a month. My goal then was to improve the gut health of both my husband and our youngest son, Jetross, who at the time constantly engaged in almost-daily arguments with his dad. Things were never the same between father and son after the ketogenic diet and juicing and loads of no-flush niacin (Vitamin B3).

On Depression-Healing Fruits

Mangoes and apples have been my favorite fruits since I was young. When I entered adulthood, I was hooked to eating *Santol* (Cottonfruit) and *Lansones* (Lanzones/Lansat).

Every year I looked forward to the 2 to 3 months that these fruits are in season and I bought as much as I could eat. As I was wrapping up the writing of this book, it occurred to me that I haven't even taken the time to find out what it was in these fruits that I gravitated to. And guess what? Both Lansones and Santol are rich in Niacin and Vitamin C, the two nutrients that go hand in hand in regulating our mood

On Plant Foods That Helped Heal My Depression

In every house that we lived in, I strived to do pot-gardening and grew our own leafy vegetables such as: *kangkong* (water spinach), *talbos ng kamote* (sweet potato tops), *alugbati* (malabar spinach), *pechay* (native cabbage) *kalamansi* (Philippine lemon), tomatoes, peppers, eggplants, okra, turmeric, herbs, etc. I had cravings not just to eat my produce but also to have my hands in the soil as often as I could.

Aside from the cooked dishes that we used the leafy vegetables in..

...we found out that we could also use them raw in smoothies in place of kale and spinach.

On Depression-Healing Restaurant Foods

Whenever we eat out, we try to go for foods that heal the gut: beef tendons, *Balut*, green leafy vegetables.

Seafoods, ox tails and feet and chicken feet.

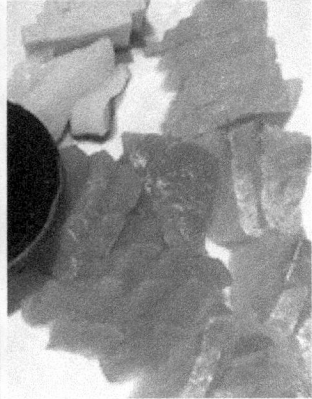

In the last photo:

Me and my family: Jetross, Jetcarl and my husband, Jet.

3 John 1-3 Living Bible (TLB)
From: John, the Elder.
To: Dear Gaius, whom I truly love.
Dear friend, I am praying that all is well with you and that your body is as healthy as I know your soul is. Some of the brothers traveling by have made me very happy by telling me that your life stays clean and true and that you are living by the standards of the Gospel.

Sickness is nature's vengeance for violating her laws.
Charles Simmons

The doctor of the future will give no medicines, but will interest his patients in the care of the human frame, in diet, and in the causes and prevention of disease.
Thomas Edison

✳ ✳ ✳

Final Words

As your gut and brain heal, you will be able to see life as it is. There are no added gloomy colors, there's no dreadful, foreboding and harrowing sounds to accompany the picture.

However, life as it is, is still difficult and perpetually demanding. As your body recovers and becomes able to face whatever stresses your life may throw at you, your ability to make the right decisions will be constantly put to the test.

Do you have the right compass to show you the correct direction to take?

"Even the securest financial plan and the finest health coverage aren't enough to hold us steady when the challenges come. We need something more, something deeper and unshakeable, something that will see us through life's hard times."
Billy Graham

As noted in Chapter 3, I entered the pit of depression as a whole being: spirit, soul and body. The trail of mistakes I made, and their ensuing consequences used up whatever remaining health I had, which then left me with the thinnest lifeline to hold on to. This is what I meant by "wolves of stresses" that undermine the integrity of our defense wall – the health of our body/gut.

Those mistakes were direct results of multiple errors in judgment which proved how far away my soul had digressed from the right path. This digression was spotlighted and revealed in all its stark nakedness by the truth of God's Word, the Bible.

The Bible is not this goofy-and-out-of-this-world-impossible-to-understand-too-spritual-jumble-of-words that some people may regard it as. **To me, it is the most practical and feasible "operations-manual-for-life-in-this-world" that's easy to understand and apply. It is the finest design for life**. (No wonder it is the best-selling book of all time with nearly 6 billion copies sold, with the 2nd in the list trailing at less than a billion!).

Without it, I proved to be utterly incompetent in maneuvering my way through life. Without it, the line that separated good from evil, and right from wrong became so murky and undistinguishable, hence my efforts to make the "right" decisions turned out futile. And without it, I would have eventually resorted to expensive professional therapy.

Repositioning my life on this divine stencil of God's will for me, that is the Bible, reaffirmed what I have known all along since I became a Christian: **that the Word of God only means well for me**; It wants the best for me because it was written by God who created me and loves me so much. The Word of God is my life's Compass and its available for you too. Let it be your "Therapist". It is mine and I sulk with it ….as often as I need.

Rose C. Manalo

Depression and Intense Anxieties: Your Quickest Way Out
A Survivor's Account
By Rose Manalo
Published by Neverbound Publishing House
74 Bel Air Drive, Cor. Fremont St., Laguna Bel Air 1, Don Jose,
Sta. Rosa City, Laguna, Region 4-A, Philippines

Twitter @rosecmanalo1
Instagram @rosecmanalo1
Facebook www.facebook.com/rosecmanalo1
Email rosalinamanalo1970@yahoo.com

Book cover image and design by Rose C. Manalo

154

Depression and Intense Anxieties Your Quickest Way Out

Medical Disclaimer:
All information, content, and material in this book is for informational purposes only and
are not intended to serve as a substitute for the consultation, diagnosis, and/or medical
treatment of a qualified physician or healthcare provider.

ISBN
Softbound/Paperback: 978-621-8153-01-1

www.ingramcontent.com/pod-product-compliance
Lightning Source LLC
Chambersburg PA
CBHW030016290326
41934CB00005B/361